The Christian Woman in the Christian Home

The Christian Woman in the Christian Home

Wilda Fancher

Broadman Press/Nashville, Tennessee

Dedicated
to
James

he makes
being the woman
in his home
such
a
nice experience

and
to
Bobby, Frank, and James Neil

they (most of the time) make
being
a
mother
a
nice
experience

Who, Indeed?

Who am I to write a book on the Christian woman in the Christian home? I, who, on occasion, and in turn—rarely all on the same day, fortunately—pout with my husband, yell at my children, neglect our parents, let down a friend, burn the toast, spend too much on a new dress, skip church at night, turn green when I visit friends in new houses, feel I'm too busy to get involved with sad-type folks. These, among other un-Christlike things, I do. Same as you do.

But I'm not satisfied with myself as a Christian. Just like you're not satisfied with yourself.

That's why I am one to write this book—and why you're one to read it. We're two who yearn for our families to look at us, but to see Christ. You could write the book as easily as I, but I'm the lucky (at this point, I'm not sure of my choice of a word here) one who got the contract.

So I'll write, you'll read, and each of us will be on our way toward being a better one—a Christian woman (or man, as the case may be) in our Christian home.

'Wilda Fancher

Reckon?

Tulips, irises, gladiolas—
  a gorgeous spring bouquet
In a tall brass vase
  on a table marked
  "In memoriam."

For me,
  to look at it is to worship.

I think of the God who made
  the flowers grow;
He made me and expects me to grow.

If I were placed in a vase
  with you and ten more Christians,

Would it be
  that for the world
  to look at us

   would be
   to worship

   the God who made us?

       'Wilda Fancher

Contents

Beginning

The June sunshine had gold-leafed the whole world for me that day. Then it traveled through the softly-stained glass windows of my church and rosy-tinted all that was in it.

Everybody else in the wedding party was in his place at the altar. Daddy and I stood waiting to hear the organist trumpet our cue. Daddy said, "Honey, I want to tell you something."

Softened by the subdued light and subdued by the rather giant step of "I do" I was about to take, I expected the revelation of the ages to come from Daddy's lips.

He said: "Every man has a hobby or something he really enjoys doing. James loves to fish. You either learn to enjoy going fishing with him or do not fuss when he goes fishing without you."

What kind of advice was that? The very last thing I was nervous about at that point was James's future fishing expeditions. I meekly said, "Yes, sir," and we took the first step of that long walk.

When I got inside the church proper and saw James, he looked quite sad. I thought, Maybe I'd best break and run and write James a note and tell him I hope he has a nice fishing trip.

About that time James looked at me and grinned widely, and I decided not to run. That was a wise decision, for I learned later that his sad expression had nothing to do with us. His face mirrored the distress he felt when he saw his mother was not wearing her orchid. It had been delivered to her home, but communication had broken down. There she sat, flowerless in front of all our wedding guests.

Daddy and I finally arrived. He gave me to James, and the

ceremony began. Dr. Howard Spell, then Dean of Mississippi College, began to speak of the nature of love. He knew us both well and knew how we needed to think of love in the marriage relationship. He looked straight into my eyes and said, "Love does not demand perfection because love cannot give perfection."

Those words have never left me.

So, on that June 11, when I became a Christian woman in my own Christian home, I got not only a husband who has proven to be a real bargain but from each of the three main men involved, I received a priceless guideline for my marriage.

From my daddy, the guideline was that I allow James to continue being himself. From James, it was that I remember the feelings of others. From Dr. Spell it was that the first thing to do to be a Christian woman in a Christian home is to scratch perfection.

If you do not have teen-agers you may think this means that perfection has an itch and you are to scratch its itch.

Not so. "Scratch" may be interpreted to mean "to sort of forget about, to sort of remove from your list of things to do for right now."

So, the first thing to do is to scratch perfection. Yours. Your husband's. Your child's.

Perfection is subjective. Therefore, it is relative, to say nothing of being nebulous. Since I'm writing this during the Mother's Day season, I'll use this holiday as an example.

Mother's Day is perfect for me if, on that day, each member of my family has his own personal life in good enough shape that he is reasonably happy and content. Presents are not important to me, but attitudes are. Evidence that the boys have healthy attitudes toward me, their daddy, each other, and themselves in the framework of a healthy total outlook on life makes Mother's Day for me. It really does not matter if their teen-age minds forget a gift or if their teen-age budgets forgot to include a gift. You might say that a healthy attitude would result in a gift. In adults it should. In teen-agers, not necessarily.

But there are mothers who feel that Mother's Day has been a total failure—all a result of their own failures—if every child does not send a card, mail a gift, call her on the phone, and come to spend the day with her.

All in between these two views there are other ideas of what a perfect Mother's Day is. So, who can say what a perfect Mother's Day is?

(Happy ending: those teen-agers I told you about did come through with a gift—a mixer, no less, *without* financing from good ole Dad.)

All perfection is equally subjective and evasive. Who can say what a perfect woman is? a perfect child? a perfect husband? a perfect home?

The second thing to do to be a Christian woman in a Christian home is to keep trying for perfection—*your* terms for perfection, *your* family's terms for perfection.

Paradoxical, you say? Maybe, but also scriptural. "Be ye therefore perfect, even as your Father."

It means to keep your eye on the perfect Father while you keep on trying to be like him.

Sometimes when I watch a family on TV and see everything turn out fine, I think, Why can't my family be like that? The answer is immediate, They follow a script; your family doesn't.

That script had been through untold revisions before it was filmed. The filming required retake after retake before it was placed in its can and marked "Ready for release." Even when it was marked that way, the director and producer probably felt it still was not as good as it should be. They saw its faults.

But when I watch the program it all seems to turn out right, mainly, because from the first concept of the story until the finished film, the people involved were striving for what they considered perfection.

Maybe they achieved some small segment of perfection, but they had to settle for something less than total perfection. However, keeping the goals of perfection in mind made it a much better piece of entertainment.

So, let's scratch perfection. Whoever decreed perfection for a woman, anyway? Wisdom, tenderness, patience, forbearance—these and other characteristics, yes. Perfection, no.

Even while we're scratching perfection, though, let's keep on trying.

I floundered around a long time trying to decide exactly what slant to give this book so far as the ages of children in the home are concerned. Finally I decided to slant it to homes where there are teen-agers. If you have small children, they will eventually be teen-agers, and you need to be getting ready for them. If your teen-agers are grown and away, you will have teen-age grandchildren one of these days. If you have teen-agers *now,* you may need help, encouragement, even company in your misery!

Recently I took the advice of some wise sage who said that the thing to do when you get to the end of your rope is to tie a knot in it and hang on. There I hung.

Screaming was not the answer. Nor was nagging. Nor was sweet-talking or begging. Somehow I was impressed there was no answer.

Everywhere I turned there was evidence that a boy had passed through, and had taken nothing with him when he departed. Left behind were ball glove, toy truck, plastic spiders, test papers to be signed, school books, yesterday's socks, even last week's apple core resting in a shirt drawer, right beside an all-day sucker wrapped in Kleenex. Everything had been left right where it landed at the expiration of its usefulness. Everything.

Not a single boy follows his dad's example of hanging up clothes. Not one boy has the slightest idea that tops will fit back on toothpaste, jars, and bottles. None has learned that doorknobs are for shutting doors as well as opening them. They interpret a doorknob as a hook, hanging coats, ties, shirts and pants three-deep on each one—after the flat surfaces are covered two-deep.

Such is the plight many mothers find themselves in. What to do?

Do like the sage said—tie a knot in the rope and hang on.

It takes just as much forbearance to put back an article a teen-ager borrowed as it does to put away a toddler's toys. It takes just as much long-suffering to get a teen-ager to put the article back as it does to get the toddler to pick up his toys.

While the ages of the children may be different, the principles and the traits of character involved are the same. In teaching a toddler to put away his toys you are really teaching several things: care of his toys, reasonable neatness for the sake of appearance, reasonable neatness for the sake of enjoyable surroundings, consideration for the mother of the family and her energy, respect for himself as a participating member of the family who carries his end of the load of making the home a reasonably orderly and pleasant place.

There are times when I get my map and look to see if there is a Walden Pond anywhere close. Tempted as I am, though, I know there is no road to Walden for me. I am a Christian woman who must relate to her world and its problems.

Like you, I brought many dreams with me to the marriage altar. Many of the dreams have come true. While some dreams come true, some don't. It's adjusting to both kinds of dreams—the did-come-true ones and the didn't-come-true ones—that makes for happiness.

Recognizing the reality of a former dream helps, too. Rejoicing in its reality is vital to mental health. While it is true that "getting there" is half the fun, "walking on by" is not to be sneezed at.

Why chase a dream if catching it does not make life sweeter?

Suppose I spent three days before Christmas cooking so that I placed a dream dinner on the table at noon on Christmas Day. Then, when my family had assembled around it, I would say, "All year you've dreamed about this Christmas dinner. I have worked at its preparation for three days. Now it is a reality. But we will not enjoy it. We will look at it and say, 'This dinner is a dream come true.' Then we will each take an armload of it and throw it in the garbage."

My family would not wait to make an appointment to take me for help. Everyone knows Christmas dinner is for looking forward to and waiting for, but even more, it is for eating and enjoying.

So is the fulfilment of dreams. Life has a million dreams. Most of them are little dreams and many of them do come true. Fault lies not with dreams but with human failure to recognize a dream come true.

Mankind is pretty much like it was since the fall of man. We still have the same basic needs and the same basic nature. The progress of the world has made more circumstances in which man must relate and control his needs and nature, but in the midst of all the changes we must weather, our revelation of God through Christ remains completely stable. It is through this revelation that we encounter the will of God for us.

It is not enough that I look at Christ and say, "There is God."

It is not enough that I look at God and say, "He is my Father."

It is not enough that I look at myself and say, "You are a child of God."

I must add, "Be ye therefore perfect even as your Father which is in heaven is perfect."

And how shall this be? It shall be at the expense of much happy energy. What is so sad about doing whatever you're doing real well? A sense of accomplishment after a job well-done makes for a much better night's sleep than furtive unease about shoddy or neglected work.

"Be ye therefore perfect even as your Father which is in heaven is perfect."

Will perfection ever be? No. Then why try? Because it is in the trying that we aim high and find we need help. A sense of companionship with and encouragement from God is the most valuable aid to achievement a Christian has.

It is the will of God that the Christian woman seeks—for herself as she helps her husband do the will of God for him, the will of

God for the house that is their home, for the children as she helps them know God so they will recognize his voice when he speaks to them and reveals his will for them.

"Be ye therefore perfect even as your Father which is in heaven is perfect."

Sounds so simple, doesn't it?

How terribly complex we make it.

Her God

Most any time I get a tomato out of the refrigerator I look it over carefully to see if it is good. If it is good, I use it.

That's what a Christian woman should do to her concept of God. Get it out, look it over carefully, and see if it is good. If it is, keep on using it. If it isn't, get a new concept.

Attendance at a concert with no knowledge of the artist, no understanding of the program, no appreciation of music will bring little joy or sense of improvement to the one who goes. A bunch of people seem to be handling their Christian journey in the same way. Failing to get a clear concept of God, his world, and his people, they stumble around and find themselves unorganized and often disenchanted with Christianity.

What does a proper concept of God include? Who he is. Where he is. How he works. Who you are in relation to him.

If you are not capable of using the Bible properly enough to find Scripture references to lead you to a real concept of God, you should get some help. A first source of help is an older, dedicated Christian woman who has wrinkles that came from smiles and wisdom that came from experiences of faith exercised through joys, sorrows, crises.

A second source of help would be a Christian woman of your own age group in whom you see an evidence of a genuinely personal relationship with God. A third one would be a pastor who has had the benefit of theological study.

Coming to this concept of your own may take many hours of study, talking, praying, thinking—maybe even some struggle within your mind and heart, maybe a little shaking up.

To believe in Christ is sufficient for a salvation experience and a sense of eternally belonging to God. For a less nervous, less fearful, less tense, less strained life now, a personal concept of God is indispensable.

I will share my concept of God with you.

Point One: God is the Creator. This is the place where I began with God. I wanted an explanation of how the world got here. Then I wanted to know how man got here. The first explanation I heard was the Genesis explanation. "In the beginning God created the heaven and the earth." And before he quit he had created everything in this world. Who knows? Maybe some other worlds, too.

Nothing I have read anywhere but the Bible or heard from any other source has given me a better explanation than that. There have been some exquisitely insane theories set forth about creation. One, beautifully presented in a secular magazine some months ago, suggested everything came from "earthroots." Whatever is an earthroot? A turnip, a carrot, maybe a potato?

Scarcely can I remember learning anything before I learned that God made the world. But I sat, a mature middle-ager, in a classroom in graduate school and listened while a man of excellent mentality began his lecture in this vein, "Before Darwin's theory, man was thought to have come about by a special creation of God . . . now we believe man very slowly evolved from an ape-like anthropoid with no learning." I rapidly took notes, disagreeing violently inside but maintaining poise outside.

What would I do if a future test question required an answer from that statement? It seemed as if the Lord said to me, "In the beginning God created the heaven and the earth and man. Do not let this man's lack of spiritual perception shake your faith." Across the lecture notes, I wrote, "Blah!" And in parentheses I wrote: I disagree with this professor. I believe God created man fully endowed physically and mentally.

Flour, butter, and sugar, salt, flavoring, baking powder, soda, and eggs do not create themselves. Set in the oven they do not emerge forty minutes later a cake without some power greater than their own. Four yards of silk, a dress pattern, zipper, spools of thread, and buttons do not create themselves and become a dress without some power greater than their own. The sun, moon, stars, earth, and myriad other elements did not create themselves and arrange themselves into a well-ordered universe without some power greater than their own.

Neither did dust of the earth nor one-celled creatures of the sea breathe into themselves the breath of life and become man without some power greater than their own. The name I believe belongs to the power that did this is God, Yahweh, as revealed in the Bible, the story of God: his world, his man, himself, presented in Genesis as the Creator.

And when others say differently, I remember that.

Point Two: After everything was created and God saw that it was all good, how did everything get so messed up? Because Adam and Eve had been created with minds of their own and the ability to make their own choices. That's what caused it all to go sour. Eve made a bad choice and Adam followed after her, but I have no rocks for Eve . . .

It was some kind of fruit
That Satan said Eve ought to eat.

She ate it.
But what if she hadn't?

Satan was bound to be man's undoing. Satan was hitting at God,
And he would have offered that fruit to the next woman he met.

If Eve had refused to eat the fruit
  Satan would have offered it to the next one,
    and the next one
      and the next one

and the next one.
      Suppose each of them refused
      And finally he had met me?

                                    —'Wilda Fancher, 1969

Point Three: I'm sure God hoped Adam and Eve and any others who were created along with them would not make the bad choice, but he must have felt he had to give them the choice, for fellowship with nonthinking beings would be quite shallow. Knowing the possibility of man's estranging himself from God, God planned for the means of removing estrangement and for restoring fellowship—the sacrifice of Jesus.

I understand the sacrifice of Jesus better when I think of our Apollo flights. In conversations about space travel all sorts of venturesome statements are likely to be heard. But not from me. My statement usually is, "There is not enough money anywhere to get me on a ship into space. There's not enough of *anything* to get me on one."

Because I live with an adventuresome bunch of guys, I have to swallow hard a lot. When the boys were little and found out I could not swim, you'd have thought I had eyes where my ears should have been, so I trotted to the "Y" every day for two weeks to learn to swim. I even had to go off the high dive the last day of the course to escape the epithet, "Chicken!"

I've let them badger me into many other uncomfortable situations. At Disneyland they conned me onto the Matterhorn, which has to be the world's most hair-raising ride. While I was slamming around inside that man-made mountain I promised the Lord if he would let me get off that hook safely I would never be so foolish again. And I haven't, either. On our second trip to Disneyland, I rode on a nice, gentle, bolted-down bench while the rest rode the Matterhorn.

The other day when I was wondering, as I often do, what does indeed spur men to space exploration, I again concurred with myself, I wouldn't go on a space ship under any circumstances.

Then, for some reason, I added, The only thing that could head me to the moon would be for one of my children to be stranded up there and the only way for him to get home would be for me to go get him.

And you know what I thought about, don't you? It wasn't a spaceship named Apollo on the moon. It was a wooden missile named cross on an earth hill called Calvary—a cross manned by Christ, my heavenly Father in the flesh, coming to get his little child and bring her home.

After the chill bumps went away, I felt deliciously warm.

Point Four: After Jesus completed the plan for my redemption, the Holy Spirit was let loose to hover around Christians, to lead them, to comfort them, and to love them for God, as much as each Christian will allow.

He dwells in every Christian. I do not have to recognize his presence to make it a reality. It *is* a reality. The happiest days for me are the days when I *do* recognize his presence and allow him to do all the nice things God sent him to do for me—things like overcoming fear, putting a worry aside, thinking of someone who needs help I can give, trusting him to watch over my children, all sorts of personal, sweet things that make life better.

There is a real sense of joy in recognizing the hand of God, his Holy Spirit, at work in my life. It makes praying a richer experience because I express more gratitude, and you know how your love grows toward someone when you're grateful.

Point Five: I belong to God. My reason for existing is to seek his will and to do it.

God has a plan for every life. He is never careless. He never misplaces his sheep. I do not have to worry at any time that he will lose me. The reason this particular trait of God's comes to my mind is that I once misplaced one of my little sheep.

I could not find Frank, the second born, anywhere. I had retraced all my steps. I had picked up all three boys, as usual, in the same place behind the school. I took Bobby by the church for choir meeting, left James Neil at the barbershop, and Frank and I came home, I was sure. Those had been the two stops I had been planning to make all day long, and I had made them.

Twenty minutes after we arrived at home, I checked to see about Frank. He did not answer my call. This, in itself, was not so unusual—some playing places were out of voice range if the wind were blowing wrong (or right). Shortly, I yelled and honked the car horn, Waiting plenty long for an answer, I soon realized none was coming. So I called the neighbor's to tell Frank to come home. He wasn't there.

That brought me to the hair-tearing stage. The boys, first-, third-, and fourth-graders, were still required to check in every once in a while as well as to get permission to leave the neighborhood. They had been quite obedient about that. So, where was Frank? I drove around the neighborhood and found all the playing places completely uninhabited.

How can you lose a boy? Over and over and over I retraced, in my mind, my trip from school. Only two stops—to leave Bobby at the church and James Neil at the barbershop.

Now, I really was uneasy. Then I convinced myself that I was being ridiculous. Wherever Frank was, he was all right.

But the fact remained, I had lost Frank. There was nothing to do but to call James and tell him I had lost one of our boys. How do you tell a man, and your husband at that, that you have lost one of his children—that you put him somewhere, but can't remember where?

Slowly I dialed 845–2227. Just as James answered I said, "Honey, I think I have lost Frank." Before he could answer, I said, "Oh, I know where I put him."

James is accustomed to this sort of fuzzy thinking from me, so he soundlessly waited while I incoherently explained that when I left James Neil at the barbershop, as I had been planning to do all day, I noticed that Frank's ears were rather high, so I had shooed him out of the car into the barbershop, too.

It was a rather funny, frightening experience. To think that my mind worked so completely one-track was frightening; the relief was so great it was funny. The worth of an experience is in the looking back at it and learning from it. Though I was dismayed at the trick my mind had played on me, my heart was lifted when I considered that God would never forget if he put me out at the last minute at the barbershop. In fact, I do not think God's plans for me are made in such haphazard fashion. I think he has them all laid out, knows them by heart, and will lead me just where I need to go. And know where he has led me every minute and every step, if I have followed.

And even if I haven't followed, he'll know where I went. Failure in the Kingdom work lies with human beings who do not find and do his will, not with God.

For I am just like Eve—I make the bad choice too often. Still, God loves me, I am forgiven through my faith in Jesus Christ, and I keep trying to be in the center of God's will.

Point Six: One of these days I will die. Everyone knows he will die sooner or later. Lots of folks come to a time when they are made to realize death may be sooner rather than later.

The surgeon was explaining to me that a tumor nestling in the muscle and nerve tissue just outside my spine indicated surgery. It was suspected of being a harmless fatty tumor, but only by actual examination could its content be determined. Arrangements were made for my entrance into the hospital two weeks later.

Some lack of ease in the surgeon's manner was almost disquieting, but not quite. Then in the last few minutes of our visit he said, quietly and seriously, something like this: " 'Wilda (he had been in college with us), I cannot let you go to surgery without telling you that there is about a 5 percent chance this tumor may be malignant. If it is, this is a mighty bad place for it to be."

Five percent had always seemed negligible. Now it loomed

mountainous. The surgeon told me that if I became too nervous about it all to call him. I assured him a full two weeks would be needed for me to get things in order (what a sinister phrase, suddenly). Besides, I whistled in the dark, I was a veritable Rock of Gibraltar—my faith would see me along.

On the way home I realized the message had come through loud and clear: a doctor had looked me in the eye and said, "You may have cancer."

I talked back and forth with myself. Self, cancer happens to other people, not to me.

Finally I said: OK, 'Wilda, why do you think you're so special that cancer can't happen to you? Where did you get some special immunization? Face it, self. You may have cancer.

So I faced it during the ride home. Then came genuine frustration—when I was trying to work out a future for my family without me, when I was facing the possibility of a slow death to which I thought I could not subject James and the boys, when I was spinning the wheels in my head toward getting the world, especially my small world, ready to carry on without me, when I was trying to keep my chin up and not quivering.

Before I reached despair, I remembered my God. I need not face this alone. "Child, don't fret. I can work it all out . . . I have already worked it out . . . don't you remember, all things work together, you know, for good."

Now, I didn't know if he meant that he would see to it that I did not die, or that he would see to everything if I did die. But I knew then that I *was* like the Rock of Gibraltar—I had not been loosened, it was just the restless water around me that made me feel as if I would topple. The assurance of God's hand still steady on my life was all I needed to settle down.

By the time I reached home with the flippant report, "I knew if I looked long enough I would find a doctor who would recommend two weeks of rest," my heart's moorings were fast in the haven of God's wise power. I never climbed the walls, nor did I lose sleep. Only once did I call the surgeon for reassurance, "Do you really think there's a 95 percent chance this tumor is not malignant?"

I think when I went to sleep for surgery I was not sure in whose presence I would be when I was next conscious. I really do not think I would have been surprised had God's eyes met mine. But they didn't. Two sparkling brown ones above an ocean-wide grin looked down at me as the dearest voice of all said, "Honey, you don't have cancer—you're going home—and you're going to be just fine. Isn't that good?"

I smiled one of those silly half-drunk smiles and said not a word. But my heart said, I'm so glad he worked it out this way instead of the other.

But one of these days I *will* die—I will go through an experience translating me from earth to heaven and into the eternal physical presence of God. An experience which accomplishes that can't be all bad.

Such is my concept of God. It makes me able to have a real gratitude for the past from which to learn and on which to build, to feel a sense of thrill and accomplishment in the present, and to hold a deeply calming hope for the future.

When I see friends who will not accept a livable concept of God and who grasp about for something that never is there, I silently consider the evidences scattered all about me, and in me, that God is.

Her Identity

Finding one's identity is not a problem which women have a corner on. Probably because our lives are so segmented and, at times, fragmented, we feel dimly outlined and hardly discernible at all.

I have had the odd feeling, occasionally, that when one of our boys said, "Hey, Mom, can you run me out to the ball field?" that he really put his fingers in his mouth, whistled, and said, "Hey, taxi!"

Or that when one said, "Mama, my watermelon-striped pants are not on the third coat hanger from the left in my closet," that he was saying, "Mrs. Dry Cleaner, your delivery boy failed to return my pants today."

Or when one said, "By the way, Mother, would you stir up one of those chocolate sheath cakes today?" that he really placed an order, "Mrs. Bakery Lady, please deliver one sheath cake by four this afternoon."

I have the sensation of groping my way out of the electric mixer and washing machine to wave a whiff of perfume at them from a white lace handkerchief and say: "Look, I'm me—a real people. See, I have not only hands and feet to work with. I have a brain to think with and a heart to feel with and a tongue to talk with. Don't you know me? I am your mother, not your mothering service."

Those feelings are the ones I have on days when I lock the keys in the car or put salt in the tea. Most days my identity is no trouble for me. It took me a while to find it, but I did find it, just as every woman must find hers. If she doesn't, her life may build itself into too big a muddle to be coped with.

Probably at first glance a woman's identity seems mixed up with more things than is a man's identity, but a second glance shows that a man's identity is mixed up with about the same. Among what must a man find his identity? Wife, children, other family, in-laws, vocation and all the people involved with it, community responsibilities, church responsibilities, political involvement, and you would probably add more to the list.

Doesn't a woman search for her identity in all of these areas? In fairness to our sex we would add to a woman's list the mechanics of running a household, making it into whatever home her family wishes it to be.

In the midst of all these demands, and others, in the Christian home we find a man, your husband, and a woman, you, hunting for yourselves. If you can look for yourselves together, things will usually work out better than if each of you goes off in separate directions. Two people coming together to make a life of all the facets of background each brings must of necessity sort themselves out.

As difficult as a long engagement period is physically, a couple serious about making their marriage permanently happy can teach each other a lot about themselves during one. They can find out how far apart they are on some ideas and how close they are on others. They can find out the dreams each has for the future and determine if the dreams can include both. A man's dream mustn't close his wife out, or her identity may be lost before they begin.

The starting point, it seems to me, with a married woman's finding her identity is with her husband. By the same token, the starting point with a man's finding his identity is with his wife. No need for either identity to get lost or be overshadowed, nor for one to become, over the years, more important. Complementary is the word.

Fulfilment in an identity is another key. This is why finding one's identity along with the other's is so important. Let's take a very easily understood example.

Suppose a girl—let's call her Judy—is engaged during her senior year in college to a young man—shall we say Tom—who already knows his life's ambition is to excel in open heart surgery. Anywhere from six to ten years of school and work past college should get him ready for his first practice. Their dates ought not be spent only in satisfying their enjoyment of being together. Judy ought to be listening to Tom's dream.

Tom should manage to take Judy to the med school where he'll go, show her the mountainous textbooks he must master and why he must master them. She should see the operating room where he will work, the room where he'll sleep when he is on duty. These things will be her archrivals for years unless Tom can help her make them a part of her identity through the part they'll play in her life, as drudgery for him right now but invaluable knowledge later. Maybe it'll be easier for her those 2,600 nights or so that Tom has more time for the books than he has for her.

Tom should also help Judy understand whatever they'll have available to supplement the love they plan to live on, for a supplement is necessary. Preferable form for the supplement to take is money. Judy may look forward to a fabulous manner of living when Tom has made the grade, but until then pickings may often be slim. Judy may need to work. Can she? Does she mind? Can she accept this as a part of her identity with Tom toward his identity as a heart surgeon? Will she resent the fatigue and loneliness just ahead?

How about children? How about a place to live? How about doing without a few of the goodies for a while? The cost of doing without is a lot higher than it was when we were coming along because the standards of doing without are a lot higher than they were then.

When Tom's ship comes in, Judy's loneliness is not over. In fact, her life will never really be her own except as she can relate it to

Tom's work. Maybe Judy and Tom would do well to visit with doctors and their wives to hear several viewpoints about the life they're getting into.

Just glibly saying with stars in her eyes, "I'll make it," is not really sufficient for a girl like Judy to say when she begins married life. Eyes ought to be wide open, goals ought to coincide with her husband's; determination to keep the air clear and communications open must find strength from both Judy and Tom. Else, the trip together should be called off.

The same process of understanding and planning can be equally helpful to a girl—shall we say Sally—engaged to a boy—who will be Jim—who did not finish high school and is serving an apprenticeship to a carpenter. It'll be a while before they see their ship, financially speaking, appear on the horizon. Living conditions for Sally and Jim probably never can be what Judy and Tom can expect. But their identities are as important for happiness on their economic level as Judy's and Tom's are for them several brackets up.

It may be that Sally and Jim have serious problems ahead unless they both accept conclusively that they are limited before they begin. Of course, Jim may have the ambition to foster a dream of his own construction company, the brain to handle it, and the elbow grease to accomplish it. In such a case, Sally has much the same path to go as Judy—years when work and business consume Jim's time and energy, when every cent possible is put back into the business. Jim and Sally must fit their identities together in such a framework.

It has been my understanding that many couples make it fine through the hard, demanding years. It seems to be at the time when they have finished the long climb to the top of the mountain that they are not able to sit down and rest with each other. Somewhere on the way an identity was lost or communication was broken down. They got to the goal, but someone was changed. Or maybe they never agreed on where the top of the mountain would be, and one wanted to keep climbing, thinking they were not there yet. Everything seems to need a framework, even one's identity. We're all more comfortable within one. The individuals who decide to get outside the framework of conformity really only build themselves another framework, nonconformity. However, a woman ought not try to mold herself into whatever image magazines and TV and news media have created as the glamorous American homemaker. They always seem to give her a mentality that will fit inside her thimble instead of her brain. Whatever other endowments they give her, glamor heads the list.

Let's face it, many are homemakers but few are glamorous. It is really quite frustrating to fit into a mold which is, in most cases, the wrong shape. Glamor suggests slender bodies; most homemakers have large bodies. Glamor suggests gliding grace; most homemakers keep such a pace we get around with the grace of a slew-footed giraffe. Glamor suggests poised hands with shining nails; most homemakers have hands that get their shine from detergent bubbles dripping off.

What's a Christian woman's identity? What means the most to her? That may be a key to her identity, assuming she is a reasonably mature woman. Identity doesn't stay exactly the same. It changes with time, with interests, with demands. Tracing one's own identity will reveal this. I'll trace mine to show what I mean.

First I was Odie and Lizzie Kate Trenor's baby. Then, for years I was Mary Lee Trenor's little sister. Nobody knew I had a name. Then I became James Fancher's wife, and now I am Bobby Fancher's mother, Frank Fancher's mother, and James Neil Fancher's mother.

But I am still the baby of the Trenor family, Mary Lee's sister, James's wife. All of these separate identities have made me *me*.

Fortunately, for my ego—and writers are egotistical, in case you did not know—all these people have on occasion been identified as a result of their relationship to me. Because I spent so many years being Mary Lee's little sister I was delighted when she was finally introduced one day as *my* sister. After that, I told James I guessed I would really be tickled if he would get introduced as my husband. One day he did. And, on various occasions the boys have been identified as being *my* sons. We have no way of getting away from each other. That suits me fine, because it is in the framework of being James's wife and the boys' mother that I find my real identity. Anything else is really beside the point. Anything else must take seacond place. For I am a Christian woman in a Christian home. That is my identity, first, foremost, and without question.

Identity means simply the state of being a specific person or thing and no other; it means one's individuality or one's distinctive character. It does not mean denouncing those who have helped to give us our distinctive character.

For a woman it's hard to get away from being a wife and a mother. Sometimes this is good. Sometimes it is bad. But it is in the framework of being a wife and mother that a woman who *is* a wife and mother must find her identity—her individuality, her distinctive character.

There shouldn't, in this day of ease, be any reason why a woman should lose her identity, individuality, and peace of mind by being cooped up at home. She should be able to be a real person as well as a mamma.

No need to let the day with the kids keep her from being able to talk with her husband that night as intelligently as she talked with him before marriage. It might not be too far wrong to say that couples have glorified or glamorized memories of their evenings of conversation before marriage. They were so enamored with each other they probably didn't talk much and when they talked, it probably involved only them.

I can't remember that James and I talked much about anything other than ourselves, our dreams, and our plans. We didn't discuss international news, the stock market, presidential campaigns, and the such. There really wasn't any world except ours.

So, what's so stupid and dumb about a husband and wife talking after supper about their children, the car repairs, the possibility of a patio? These are the realities of this world they dreamed about, planned for (or let happen), and spent their evenings poring over before they were married. It should be no less enchanting than it was then.

If current-event knowledge is necessary for stimulating conversation, such knowledge is as close as the TV or kitchen radio. Nothing has to be neglected in order for a woman to listen to what's going on in the world. Reading about it is another matter, though. That does take time, which may not be too plentiful.

A woman's personality need not be sacrificed during the years her home responsibilities are so heavy. She can have a good life which can include something outside her four walls. A woman may find that activity outside her home enriches not only her life but her whole family's. If there is something that brings a relief from tension, smile lines may replace the frown lines on her face. If it gives a break in the pace, it may put a lift in her step.

If work outside the home is necessary, or simply desired, then the identity problem has another facet. Even then it does not seem unreasonable to expect that a woman who is a wife and a mother should still find her identity in relation to her family. A Dr. Jekyll and Mrs. Hyde sort of thing can play all manner of havoc with family emotions. A family should not be made to feel that they are so dull that Mamma must find something else to keep her spirits up. If a Christian woman has the responsibility of a family, it is their well-being which should come first.

The family is the unit in which the Christian home exists. While people of other persuasions than Christianity may discard the "custom" of marriage, bearing and rearing children outside the framework of responsible legality, the sanctity of marriage will hallow the homes of followers of Christ.

A family has many functions, all of which have been defined and analyzed at length by various kinds of scholars. Most of the functions of a family make possible three very important things:

1. A husband and wife living together in a way that makes life for both of them so much better than living alone that they could not even consider living apart.

2. Replenishing the earth with legitimate babies.

3. Rearing the babies in the nurture and admonition of the Lord, preparing them to be able to establish a home when they have grown up.

All the things that go on in a home must be helpful to every member of the family. If anything is harmful to any member in the home, then the family is not doing what it should. This description of a family seems to anticipate perfection, Utopia, and heaven all rolled into one. It's the keeping on trying for just such a situation that makes homes better and better.

The success of the next generation has its basis in the success of the family unless outside influences are allowed to usurp the place of the family. Some psychologists are now saying that the home is less than a third responsible for the production of well-adjusted adults because so many factors outside the home bring such force to bear, even on small children.

Maybe in this place lies a mother's most important privilege—protecting her children while they're small, defending them by teaching and explaining lasting truths to them as they grow and must, because of educational needs, leave the home for long days, and by informing herself correctly and positively so that her teaching will be valid.

Understanding the needs of her family is the first homework a mother must do. This begins with her husband. She has him first, and his needs must be learned first.

Her second assignment is figuring out how she can fill the specific needs. The last, and toughest assignment is disciplining herself to be what she must be to fill the needs.

While examining the needs of her family, a woman must remember that she is a member of the family and include her needs when she's planning. However, I believe we would agree that if, even after careful planning, anybody's needs must be slighted, it should be the mother's. This does not mean she should flatten herself into a door mat for the family's feet. But it does mean that a great deal of selflessness is helpful to a mother.

A family needs from each other many things: love, instruction, trust, laughter, help with tasks, sympathy, patience, forbearance, loyalty, understanding, smiles, tenderness, gentleness. All of these things take time. How is a mother going to know why her son's grades suddenly fell if the family hasn't had time to talk about how the son is not being given a chance to bat at batting practice, even though he has always played good baseball.

How's a father going to know why his children recently lost respect for one of their men teachers if there has not been enough conversation to know that the teacher has belittled and embarrassed some of the Negroes newly court-ordered into school?

A family must have time together, and the woman is the one to insist on it and to arrange for it. And it isn't easy.

Most of a family's time seems to be taken up with making money. This may be OK as long as everybody has the right idea about money and there is time together for something else. Husband and wife time is necessary; whole family time is good; parent-child time pays great dividends; children time together helps them know each other better.

The needs of the family members dictate when and how this time should be taken and how it should be spent. Some folks have been able to find an answer in taking the same times every week for one or more of these kinds of times. Probably a set, uninterfered-with time is fine for husband and wife time.

Parent-child time or whole family time should be flexible to do for the child what the child needs done. There is no way to predict when a child may be snubbed by a friend and need something sort of special to help him through a bad time. We do not, of course, say, "Honey, I'm sorry John snubbed you, so we're going to drop everything and go to the Mall."

Instead, "I believe if you will allow a sandwich supper, Dad and I (or only one, if better) will have time to run to the Mall with you and check on that sport coat you were interested in," may lift spirits high enough to let air in to heal the wound.

A stockpile of things the young person likes to do, wishes he had, places he wants to go ought to be programed so thoroughly in the computer of your heart that something can be pulled out so subtly to help a child through a hard time he'll not recognize your maneuvering.

Family structure is important—this is a sort of struggle for each member to find his place. Parents often have a hard time deciding the structure. We are likely torn between the desire to be buddies and to be wise parents. Too firm a hand may produce fear in amounts too large for a properly growing child to handle. Too lax a hand may produce confusion in amounts too large for him to handle.

Somewhere between authoritarianism and permissivism there is the happy medium of gentle, steady parental guidance. Such guidance must be accented, on rare occasions, with authoritarianism. It is not a breach of a parent's intelligence nor an insult to a child's when parental authority is exerted without explanation or apology.

This may sound extreme, but all who have teen-agers know that there are times when a teen-ager does not accept a parent's explanation or reason as plausible and logical. When a parent, on the basis of previous conversation, knows his reasons are held invalid by the child, he has no choice but to act like a parent.

It takes dedication to the task to know how a parent should behave, to know what to do. All of this is a part of a Christian woman's identity.

A woman likes to feel that her life is a column of figures—a figure added for each stage of her life—all to be added and found adequate. Sometimes she tries to add too many figures by taking on too many jobs or by placing herself too far outside the framework of her family.

A woman needs to be conscious of herself, needs to know herself, needs to learn about being a woman. She needs to help her husband and children know her. All need to have some idea of the way she clicks.

A woman must be careful or she will obliterate herself, and nobody will miss her until it is too late.

An identity crisis, where a woman may find herself from time to time, is a time of intensive feeling about oneself and what to do with oneself. This is oversimplified, I guess, but maybe we over-complicate too often. An identity crisis isn't a one-time happening. It keeps cropping up. We keep stumbling into the darkness. If one has the proper spiritual lighting, she makes it through each crisis with safety and will find joy in each progression of her identity, from childhood to infinity.

But a woman must be honest with herself about who she really is. Here's what I mean.

At our house everyone has his own closet. Luxurious arrangement, wouldn't you say? No member of the family is allowed to encroach upon the privacy of other closets. I tried. But James said there was no way—considering the absolute simplicity of drying his ten hairs—to justify the one square foot my hair dryer sat upon in his closet. He had to nag me a little (six months isn't long), but I moved it out.

The closets are odd-shaped, probably the oddest-shaped collection of closets to be found in our town. But they function as closets do. *Not* as closets *should,* but as closets *do.* Conglomerate and pack-rattish in appearance, each closet serves as a receptacle for anything which cannot be stuck beneath something else, pushed behind something else, or stuffed into something else when I deliver the ultimatum: "This messy way of life will end *today.* Clean up your room!"

With a private closet for each of the four men in the house you would think my closet would be filled with sugar and spice and everything nice, wouldn't you? Guess what blocks my reach, at least once a week, of the rack on which I hang my clothes? Guns, rifles, 410's, 22's.

Guess what makes the rattling sound on the floor of the closet if I'm not very careful when I get a purse or pair of shoes off my closet shelf? Shells, red and green and tan shotgun and rifle shells falling off *my* shelf.

I never go hunting. I never target practice. In fact, I never shoot the guns. That is not to say that I am not tempted. I know the reason whoever was in charge of setting up the original gun rules put at the head of the list, "Never keep a loaded gun in the house." He knew that by the time a mother took time to load a gun she would have got the upper hand of the temptation to shoot her teen-ager.

Closets are great in theory, but impossible in practice.

Sometimes I feel like a closet. Like a rack loaded with clothes which need mending or freshening. Like shelves cluttered with unimportant things that ought to be thrown away. Like a floor cluttered with a bunch of junk that nobody has use for. Like a space filled with laziness, uselessness, and trivia. I feel like a closet because I close the door to hide the mess of me and give an outward appearance of industry, usefulness, and importance.

But when I'm honest with myself and with God, I know that if I feel like a closet, I must feel like a closet that has been through spring housecleaning. Because God sees me all straight and in order behind the door called Christ.

What more identification can a Christian woman need? It makes me want to sing all day long while I'm being who I am.

Her Housekeeping

What's the point of housekeeping, anyway? By the time the dishwasher—if you're lucky—finishes cleaning the breakfast dishes, the table must be set for lunch. Supper follows practically on lunch's coattail. If you feel like I do, at least once each week or so you have to talk yourself out of accidentally dropping every dish you own because you are sick of looking at them and tired of handling them.

No sooner have you folded the last clean clothes than Wise Guy No. 1 walks in and demands to know where his chartreuse socks are—they couldn't possibly still be dirty: he hasn't worn them since last night. That causes you to jab your finger with a needle you're using to sew a button back on the gold shirt; then Wise Guy No. 2, owner of the shirt, notices that the pants he intended to wear with the gold shirt haven't been sewn up yet, though he reported the damage nearly an hour ago. So, it becomes necessary for you to iron his red, white, and blue jeans because they won't go with the gold shirt; anyway, he'd already decided to wear the red shirt which the jeans match.

The blue socks to match really have been in the dirty clothes two days, so you rummage in every guy's sock drawer to find a pair of white ones. When you see the one red polka dot on the left sock just above the ankle bone, you are astounded. Then you realize it came from your bleeding finger. Quickly, before coagulation sets in, you squeeze a matching polka dot onto the right sock. Fortunately, the wise guy is young enough to feel nostalgic about the recent blood-brother pacts and finds the two dots "neat-o."

Not so with Wise Guy No. 3. He sees no gourmet qualities in cold grits and congealed fried eggs, which is what his breakfast turned into while you were icing 59 cupcakes. Your Wise Guy No. 2 told you at eleven o'clock last night he had said you would send them to school today for his club members to sell to raise money for the club's pen-pal class in Alaska to buy paint for their totem pole.

You never catch up, you never get through, you can't keep everybody satisfied. So, what's the point of housekeeping, anyway? At the risk of being elementary in defining such a monumental task as housekeeping, I'd say the point of housekeeping is to provide a house to keep a family in—the management of such a household in all its glorious tasks and affairs.

There must be an average of at least six hours a day of sheer drudgery in housekeeping; consequently, there are a few chores a woman must tend to which I am glad science is doing something about. Like ironing. I suspect my Granny Trenor and Mama Brown would have never believed, during all the hours they stood and sculptured with their irons white shirts which could stand alone, that their granddaughter would shame the name of womanhood by sending her preacher-husband into the pulpit—Sunday after Wednesday after Sunday—in a shirt free of starch and untouched by an iron. Needless to say, I am pleased as peaches I lived so long. I am so pleased, in fact, that often I actually grin as I place those lovely unwrinkled shirts and pants on hangers, and sometimes I stick out my tongue at my iron as I pass it on the way to my husband's and sons' closets, arms laden with hangersful of eternally pressed clothing.

At the same time, it was from the lowly ironing board, coupled with the even lowlier dishpan, that I learned one of the highest lessons about being a woman. The only two duties about housekeeping that I dislike are ironing and dishwashing. And who, of the vintage that I am, could "set up housekeeping" and begin to rear a family without an abundance of each? Nobody.

So I had to come to grips with each. My earliest solution was to let each go undone just as long as there was another clean dish and another ironed shirt or pair of jeans. It was a very unsatisfactory solution.

Things slid along. I'm sure that my heavenly Father was a bit outdone with me about my attitude. I think he knew I needed to be given a new outlook. I further think he knew I'd have to be *given* it, that I would wallow in self-pity forever and make no effort to change my own attitude. Consequently, I think it was his Spirit which caused my mind to function as it did on a certain day after I had been ironing.

The two oldest boys, about five and six then, were dressing to accompany some friends to a neighboring city for a movie. They were quite delighted, and I was summoned several times to help. The place from which they summoned me was the ironing board because the shirts they wanted to wear had not been ironed and I was in the hurried process of ironing them before time to go. All our frenzied efforts came out even and the results were two very fine-looking, well-groomed boys who gave every evidence of being well-cared for. My heart panted twice—once, from rushing, second, from joy.

As I watched them gleefully pile into Betty's car, something— the Holy Spirit, I plainly suspect—filled my mind with thought: 'Wilda, how can you despise something that has such marvelous results? When you are ironing, why can't you look beyond the ironing board and see your boys walking off—to school, church, anywhere, everywhere, into life? By then they were out of sight of my eyes but not out of sight of my heart. I glanced upward and said: "Thanks, Father. I needed that. I'll try to remember."

No miracle had been wrought that sent me rushing hilariously nor regularly to the ironing board, but the drudgery had been eased. I no longer saw the clothes as I laid them out before me on the ironing board. I saw them on my family, coming to life.

Because now I was able to look beyond the ironing board. And soon I could see beyond the dishpan, too.

The young bride who looks at the mess she must spend the morning with after her loving husband goes to work is often brought to tears by looking. Whoever told a bride how to go about cleaning up the mess that sleeping, bathing, dressing, cooking and eating make in a place, small though it be?

One of her wedding presents was not a book called "Ten Easy Lessons to Become a Housekeeper." That's good, because ten easy lessons would not get the job done. Maybe ten hard lessons would be more believable.

Girls ought to be trained for housekeeping; so should boys. Mothers ought not glibly say, "Oh, she'll learn when she has to." Learning ought to be done when its consequences might not be so devastating.

Maybe mothers don't teach their girls the arts of housekeeping because they themselves have never felt a sense of accomplishment in it. Maybe if they try to teach the girls, they do so with such boredom of spirit that girls reject the knowledge. If every girl could have a few weeks with a really good housekeeper—one who really enjoyed keeping house and knew how to go about it—she would spend an invaluable apprenticeship.

Efficiency experts have found no way to peddle their wares to homemakers. Nobody punches a time clock or observes any of the other efficiency-producing techniques such experts recommend. There's no such thing in the home as a typing pool. Family members do not run on a strict schedule or go by a script.

Nor should they. Home ought to be a place of refuge, a haven, a storm shelter, a foxhole, an ivory tower, a place to go. It's up to you to achieve this sort of set-up. How? When your house is overrun by faulty human beings rushing in and out and up and down, pushing each other around, yelling at each other, and generally behaving like members of a family?

By hard, steady, disciplined work. that's how. By making up your mind to. That's how. By accepting this as your best mission in life. That's how. By letting God's Spirit help you. That's how.

A favorite saying among our group of preacher friends is, "He's nervous and thinks he's busy."

These friends are dedicated, hard-working pastors, each having always led his church in vigorous programs of work. One of these friends is a particularly highly energetic human being. During a time when he was leading his church in a thorough financial campaign, an elderly little lady in the church said, to him, "Brother Simmons, you just *have* to be doing *something,* don't you?"

Maybe that's how we women are about our housekeeping. Nervous, and think we're busy. Thinking we just have to be doing something that will make us wear the badge "good housekeeper." Maybe we're afraid a neighbor will drop in and find us playing with a child instead of folding the pile of clothes in the middle of the bed. Afraid someone will think we are a poor housekeeper. Worse still, afraid to admit to ourselves that we are a little less than perfect.

Remember, we scratched perfection? That goes for housekeeping, too.

Being busy is often a frame of mind. It isn't necessarily true that being busy all the time is the answer to the hectic schedule most of us keep. Just because our nearest neighbor or best friend feels that to be adequate in her housekeeping a woman must wax her floors once a week, we often accept her standards as ours even though we really do not feel that way about floors at all. Maybe our family doesn't, either, but they have to accept the friend's standards, too, because we have.

This is not the way to arrive at your plan for housekeeping. You and your family alone should be the ones to say what your standards of housekeeping are to be.

There are some basic elements of housekeeping that a Christian housekeeper will surely strive for—sanitation, of course, reasonable neatness, and such. But past those, it is every family for itself.

I constantly face the danger of making our house a place to be approved by transients instead of by the residents. The transients have their own home. It appears to me it's the residents who should say how clean and straight this house should be.

Sometimes even a mother has to bend a bit about the housekeeping. I started out entirely too clean. When the babies came along quickly and on schedule, I decided germs were not for them. It took me a while to accept the fact that boys and dirt go together. When I accepted it, I did so with reservations. Boys and dirt might go together but they did not have to *stay* together.

Consequently, I separated them from their dirt and dirty clothes several times a day, proportionately increasing the number of rings to be washed out of the tub and the number of washers of clothes to be laundered, to say nothing of the proportionate drain on my energy and good nature.

I further decided that our house was not to be scattered with playthings—this meant constant nagging. Finally, I decided that two daily pickup times would ease the tension between the boys and me. Thereafter, all of us chipped in right after lunch and put toys, books, and so forth in place. Then bathtime (only if really necessary) was followed by resttime. We followed the same ritual after supper, and it worked quite beautifully. The boys did not pull out as much junk as they had before, but they still got just as dirty.

This is just one example of how a woman must come to grips with herself about her family and their house. There is no way for one of us women to say what is exactly right for another woman in this regard. It is vital, however, for each woman at fairly regular intervals to take stock of the atmosphere and the attitudes inside her house. A few questions might be answered in her inventory.

1. Who lives here? The same people as at the last inventory, probably, but their ages, interests, activities, abilities, responsibilities change as time goes by, so the function of the house does, too, along with the mother's role.

2. What do the people who live in the house want from their physical surroundings? One of our boys told me one day when I had really cleaned his room to a shine that he did not like it because it did not seem friendly when it was so neat and clean. A person's room really ought to make *him* feel good to be in it.

3. Is there really any need to fret over everything about the house that I fret over? Is it really worth the fretting?

4. Are we relatively happy here? Don't forget to allow for normal fussing and grumpiness of each family member. Remember, we have scratched perfection.

Pencil and paper have long been my therapy and my counselor. I have sorted many things out by praying that the Lord would help me as I sat and wrote how I felt—or didn't feel—about something.

It might work for you. Paper and pencil are all it takes. Write down your title, "What Really Bothers Me Is . . ." Then write down everything you think about—argue with yourself, even. Be fair and look at both sides. Mince no words—it's all going into the wastebasket when you're through, anyway, except the new, clear-cut understanding you've agreed with yourself on about the issue under discussion.

Sometimes you have to get real specific and work out such questions as, What is more important right now? It may be choosing between a club meeting and preparing a good dinner because you know your husband has had a hectic week so far.

Sure, the club meeting has been on your calendar for every third Thursday for three years, and your husband knows that, so he shouldn't expect anything more than a hamburger.

But on this particular third Thursday maybe the club meeting is not a priority item. Maybe the aroma of his favorite dinner greeting your husband when he comes in dog-tired, maybe discouraged, maybe dejected, maybe insecure in his job is the most important thing in your family's life today.

However, if you can't give up your club meeting and can't get away from the thought that you really should have his favorite dinner, maybe you can postpone the project you'd planned for the morning—defrosting the refrigerator. Use the morning to get the special dinner going, split to your club, and come back home to finish dinner by the time he gets home. A few times of being pampered like this, and he may buy you a frostfree refrigerator. Not that you would be guilty of ulterior motives, of course.

Flexibility (a fancy word for a woman's unquestioned prerogative, the ability to change your mind) is the key to good housekeeping. There are some things that can never be eliminated from a good housekeeper's tasks, but they can be shuffled around easily if the well-being of a family member—and that includes mother —requires.

Planning is the key to flexibility. On any given day a housekeeper can make a list of things to be done that will extend into next month even if she works nonstop. Making a list is not equal with planning.

Planning is making a scheme or method or design for the attainment of some object—a mode of action. Planning involves an intention or purpose.

What is the object of housekeeping toward which you are planning? Is it simply to fulfil the desire you have to feel you are a good mother or wife? Is it to secure your own satisfaction? Or is it to maintain a refuge for everyone who lives there—a place where he can know he is loved, protected, and provided for? This should be the object of your planning, and your planning should be flexible.

Many frustrations can be completely avoided by planning. I cannot think of any single area that needs the degree of planning that your family's meals need. Meals happen to every family three times a day, more or less. If these meals are planned in detail and the food for them for a week at a time is in the house, you face twenty-one fewer frustrations that week. These meals should be planned with several things in minds: the budget, nutritional requirements, the schedule of every family member. On the night the guy who doesn't like chicken spaghetti will be gone, plan for the rest of the family to enjoy chicken spaghetti.

Conveniences are great, aren't they? But have we really learned how to profit most from them? I'm not sure exactly where sociologists—or whoever is responsible for such things—have the brackets enclosing middle age now. However, I'm sure I'm inside the brackets, wherever they are. I'm also sure I'm leading a crusade to raise the top of the bracket a year at a time annually on August 22.

I am startled every day when I look in the mirror and have to say, "Hello, self. Another day, another wrinkle. Another day, another hair's gray."

The time between these greetings seems to get shorter and shorter. Lately I've wondered if there is some sort of secret experiment with shortening the days going on. If so, let me say to whom it may concern, the experiment is successful at our house. Nights are even shorter—should they get much shorter, I may have to resort to my Granny Trenor's strategy of a nap after lunch. Wonder how old she was when she started afternoon naps?

Part of the problem lies with all the modern inconveniences my affluent society has dumped on me. Things like burned-out dryer, clogged-up washing machines, flickering televisions, leaky faucets, and souped-up skillets leave me immobilized too much of the time.

Sometimes I think the good ole days might have been the stuff, after all. Mamas *had* to

wash all day Monday
iron all day Tuesday
clean house all day Wednesday
sew all day Thursday
cook all day Friday
go to town all day Saturday
enjoy church, family, friends all day Sunday.

It took a whole day to get each of these done, what with rub boards, twelve-pound irons to heat in the fire, brush brooms for sweeping, peddle sewing machines, wood stoves, horse and buggies, and hallowing the sabbath.

As it is now we wash, iron, clean house, sew, cook, and go to town all day every day because we have the gadgets to make this possible. We exhaust ourselves trying to bring our little world to perfection every single day.

And we still don't have enough time for family, friends, and church. All my gadgets are fine. If I could just learn to use them as conveniently as Granny did without them, I'd have it made. Maybe we sometimes try too hard for perfection.

Two questions are good to ask at the end of a day. What did I spend my time and energy on today that really was *not* important? What important thing did I leave undone that I could have done in the time I spent on the unimportant item?

Chances are that some nights you will be at odds with yourself over some wasted time.

But chances are, also, that some days you'll be able to answer the first question smugly, "Not a thing." And you'll feel good that night.

With all that is required of her strength, the Christian woman gets tired. I tried to put two empty Dr. Pepper bottles in the dishwasher this morning. We figure if one kid wants to drink Dr. Pepper with his grits and butter and salt and pepper, bacon and blueberry muffins, and if another one wants to drink Dr. Pepper with his cantaloupe, sausage and toast, that's their problem. My problem is putting the bottles in the dishwasher.

Being the perennial receiver of "The Volunteer*ed* of the Year" frays a mother's mind. Not the honor (?) of it, but the responsibilities of it. Like remembering who's supposed to be where when— whether the boy I sent to the piano lesson is the one who should have been sent to the dentist, whether the one I left in the doctor's waiting room is the one who has fever, and whether I put the cake in the oven or the dryer.

And wondering why my hair drooped, then realizing I sprayed it with bathroom cleaner instead of hair spray. If I had taken time to look in the mirror, I'd have seen the white foam. There really ought to be a federal law that all hair spray be in red cans, all bathroom cleaner in blue cans, etc.

Every day I think, Tomorrow cannot be this busy. And just like your tomorrow, it was busier. What's a woman to do when she stays so busy she can't keep her thinking straight? There's not much I am doing that I can stop, and you more than likely are in the same situation. I have already stopped doing so much that if the government inspected homes the way it does restaurants, it would close ours.

What to do about the exhaustion that drenches us? Well, I have learned a lesson from our Siamese cat. A dozen or so times a day that cat, who thinks he's a people and bears the high-sounding name "Siegfried" but is always addressed as "Cat," rests in a dozen or so different places and positions. I have watched him wiggle, turn, move, stretch, plop, and curl into an exactly right position for resting.

I don't mean to sound irreverent, but I have learned to take little catnap rests with God. It's scriptural. Not the catnap part, but the resting part. Jesus said, "Come to me when you are tired, and I'll help you rest." I don't think he minds if my Siamese cat's example helps me come to him easier.

Several times a day I momentarily position myself into the presence of God. Maybe after I make up a bed I sit down on it, considering the things that are important to the boy who sleeps in that bed and ask God to show his will about those things.

Maybe after I hang clothes in a boy's closet I stand there and thank God for the strong body which wears those clothes, remembering anxious hours about his health. Maybe after I've signed a boy's test paper I shiver a little as I pray for the mind of that boy to be protected from drugs and alcohol and faulty ideologies.

Maybe when James takes unusually seriously the problems of one to whom he ministers, I thank God for his compassionate heart but pray for some kind of spiritual platformate to be added to his emotional strength to make it run further than the problem.

Maybe when my day seems impossible I hear Jesus' command, "Come here, and I'll help you rest," in these ways: "Put your head down on your desk and think of me." "Sit in your favorite chair for five minutes and consider my strength. It becomes yours for the asking." "Curl up on the couch and loll around in forever. That's how long I'm with you."

So, I obey. I rest. In him.

Then I can see that b-a-t-h-r-o-o-m c-l-e-a-n-e-r does not spell "hair spray." And I look in the oven, where, sure enough my cake is, and it's rising.

What are the physical needs housekeeping provides for a family? First, shelter—dry, warm, cool, reasonably clean. Second, clothing —clean, mended, available when needed. Third, food—cooked, served, expected to be eaten.

Every morning the first week of school in the 1970–71 session when we made the bedroom rounds asking what each occupant would like for breakfast, the percentage of answers which sounded something like "Ugh—*nothing*" was roughly 95.6. We wheedled and pled and got a few choking morsels down unwilling throats.

There had to be a better way.

When our boys go out the door each morning to begin a school day, they go into a world as full of good and evil as the one we adults walk out to face each day. A school day is no small matter. Students have good days; the adults at school have good days. Students have bad days; the adults have bad days. When a student who is having one of his bad days and an adult who is having one of his bad days get together, it can be rough for both.

One of the first things I learned about boys—and I expect it goes for girls, too—is that their ability to be gotten along with is in almost direct proportion to the fulness of their stomachs. Keep a boy's stomach full and you're halfway there.

So early the second week, James and I declared war on the breakfast ughs. The arms for our battle were a conglomeration of favorite foods and drinks.

We announced that every member of the family would be present for breakfast at 7:30 the next morning. We got reactions like: "I just can't hack getting up early enough to get to the table at 7:30." "I just can't possibly be ready by 7:30." "Why so early?"

To the first two reactions we said, "Well, you'd better give it a tussle," and, "OK. We'll compromise—we'll get you up at seven until seven instead of fifteen 'til and have breakfast at 7:35 instead of 7:30." To the third one we said, "So you can get to school on time."

The next morning wasn't easy. It looked as if, in spite of the cantaloupe, bacon, grits, eggs, catsup, toast, jelly, coffee, milk, and Dr. Pepper on the table, that the ughs would win. Finally every boy arrived at the table, looked it over and sat down. They said not an ugh and left very few crumbs.

The next morning was easier. Smelling blueberry muffins cooking didn't slow the boys down any. It got easier every day. The ughs didn't win a single skirmish in our war against them. It was mostly a matter of our (James and I both hustle into the kitchen for all this morning madness) doing like the third little pig and getting a huge, good breakfast, complete with ice water, on an attractively set table ahead of the ughs.

Though we won the war, there was one casualty. Our food budget remains in grave condition after a full school year of these big breakfasts (and by the time this reaches you another year of them will nearly have gone by).

The point is, a child or a teen-ager does not always know what he wants, and he may say he wants no food. But its availability usually changes his mind. Good food is vital for a teen-ager. A Christian woman in a Christian home must provide the vital things for her children.

Work must go on in a Christian home, so a good attitude toward work needs to be worked out. All of me just won't grow up. I still shake and punch on my Christmas gifts because I cannot abide not knowing what they are. I still pinch icing off the cake. If it weren't for people saying, "Well, Mrs. Fancher finally finished flipping," I'd love to go skating on the sidewalks in our town.

When the winter sky sports a cloud, I'm the first to say, "I surely hope it snows." And I still like to blow bubblegum bubbles.

But lots of me has grown up, and life is easier because of that.

When I was a little girl and I heard talk about the abundant life, I really thought it meant Christians were supposed to have big houses and cars and all the trappings to go with them. I did not put away that childish thought as early as I should have, I fear. But I did finally get it put away by a very definite process of deliberation upon the thought of how a Christian can exist in such a world as this. And behave herself like she should. Especially a busy Christian woman in a Christian home.

A helpful part of God's Word in my Christian adolescence is the statement in Ecclesiastes 3:12, " . . . it is God's gift to man that every one should eat and drink and take pleasure in all his toil" (RSV).

And it has what seems to be a companion verse in 1 Corinthians 10:31: "So, whether you eat or drink, or whatever you do, do all to the glory of God." We're told what to do—eat, drink, work— and how to do it—to the glory of God.

Understanding glory is necessary. Without waxing too theological (as if I could), we might simplify glory as "distinguished honor or praise or exalted opinion." It is whatever we do ought to make the reputation and honor of God more secure in the world's eyes. Seems to me a Christian woman on an assembly line in a factory ought to do her best not just for her reputation, but for God's, to whom her fellowworkers know she belongs. Seems to me a Christian mechanic should take the same joy in repairing cars. So should a Christian young person feel about his work in school. And a mother about her work at home.

I think it was Hambone who said he would be glad to work if he could find any pleasure in it. The Bible says for us to do just that. Pleasure is defined as an agreeable sensation. Maybe the agreeable sensation doesn't always come during the work but sometimes with the result of the work.

A woman practices much as a doctor does. When a doctor begins his practice he simply digs in and faces every illness or case that comes to his waiting room. Dull ones show up. Nothing more challenging than red ears and throats may show up for several days.

Then one day his perseverance in achieving readiness rewards itself magnificently as he distinguishes symptoms of meningitis from those of a simple virus. After proper treatment works the child's recovery the physician sits back and enjoys being a doctor.

On the day when he misses the key symptoms and his nurse orders flowers for a funeral, he sits back, miserable in his failure, and hates being a doctor.

What woman among us has not come to the end of one day elated with being a woman and on the next day hated the whole business?

In our day home almost has to be a frame of mind as well as a locale. A member may dwell in the home a great deal more in mind than in body.

No time and energy have been better spent than that which causes a husband or child to carry away from home a subconscious looking forward to being back at home.

That's when housekeeping has succeeded.

Her In-Laws

All around our world struggles over men are going on. Among the fiercest is the struggle between the mother of a man and the wife of the man. The need for choosing up sides is eliminated. Placed on one side by blood and love is the mother; placed on the other side by law and love is the wife. Somewhere between these two stances is the man. He is the battleground.

Skirmish after skirmish takes place over him, and in him. To the victor belong the spoils, and spoils indeed are too often the real remains.

A spoil is a damaged thing, often damaged beyond repair. A spoil is what has happened in a too-high percentage of in-law relationships.

Nobody meant for it to. The trouble is, nobody meant for it *not* to. That is, the people involved in in-law relationships do not usually prepare themselves for those relationships.

Getting along with in-laws ought to be just about like getting along with everyone else in the world. The first thing to do is to forget the tradition that has stereotyped in-laws. Take the time to get to know your future in-laws. It does not hurt at all for in-laws to be included in the wedding plans. After all, it's their child's wedding, too.

A second thing to do is to remember that you are not always right. You may have to change your way of thinking. Third, be grown-up in your dealing with in-laws. Don't revert to childishness. Fourth, keep in mind that you tire of nearly everyone sometime. That includes in-laws.

Fifth, air your feelings in a nice way. Remember that healthy arguments can clear the way to good understanding. Perfect agreement is impossible, but it is wrong for a person who disagrees to be made to feel he or she is stupid.

Sixth, criticism of one in-law to another is absolutely taboo. The one listening will figure he'll be the object of your criticism to anyone who'll listen to you talk about him.

In-laws are people. The same rules of courtesy, thoughtfulness, kindness, decency, consideration, and concern apply to them as to other people.

Families have a much harder time being together than they used to have, especially when in-laws have swelled the ranks. Affluence probably has a lot to do with this. Everyone is quite busy working harder to have more. Mothers are working. This leaves little time and energy for preparing for and receiving company. It also leaves little time for being company.

Places to eat out are numerous. Families could go dutch on eating out when visits are exchanged. The visitor might take part of the food. Agreement on simple food, all sorts of possibilities about this are available for trying. Lack of time for food preparation and cleaning up after meals probably is one of the biggest drawbacks to families getting together.

Another factor of affluence may hinder, too: envy of the success of a brother or of a sister's husband. Members of families must compete with each other but must remain families and find fellowship together as in-laws.

In-law relationships seem to follow a pattern. The good ole daddy-in-law usually gets along fine with everybody his child inherited at the wedding. Rarely does a father-in-law figure in conflict; furthermore, he is quite likely to try to keep his wife out of the young folks' hair. Maybe he is busy so much of the time he doesn't have time to get involved in someone else's business. At the risk of alienating some readers, I will put forth the suggestion that the real reason for this is that fathers do not have to feel as indispensable as mothers do. Too, fathers have the notion—and a good one, at that—that children grow up into adults—and good ones, at that.

Brothers-in-law also cause little conflict. These two observations keep trying to say something to me, and I keep refusing to listen. If I listened, I might have to agree that men are easier to get along with than women.

Second from the top in the cause of conflicts are sisters-in-law. It seems that all sorts of things, mostly competitive and material in nature, cause jealousy, envy, resentment, hurt feelings when there is a sister-in-law around. Here a Christian concept of material possessions is the answer.

Have you guessed who is first on the list of in-law conflict? Well, most folks say it is the mother-in-law, but I'm not sure that's right. Chances are that daughters-in-law and sons-in-law should share honors with her in a tie for first.

The complaint most mothers-in-law make is that their son-in-law or daughter-in-law is thoughtless and indifferent. The mother-in-law wants to feel close to her youngster's new spouse. Possibly this is the first fallacy—looking for an even closer relationship to the two of them than she had with the one before the marriage.

The daughter-in-law and mother-in-law relationship is the most difficult. This is understandable because it involves the love, though of different natures, of two women for the same man.

It is hard for a mother to fill out a release form and hand it to her new daughter-in-law, no matter what a good catch the girl is.

A young wife may likely feel that her mother-in-law is like Moby Dick—seen and heard blowing everywhere. She was when her son was a baby, a child, a boy, a man; now, when he is a married man, she hardly can be expected to change.

If a son has turned out to be fine (and he must have, or you wouldn't have married him?), a mother feels responsible and feels that her guidance and advice must continue if he is to continue to be fine. Quite logical thinking, wouldn't you say? It is too sudden a reversal of roles, this changing from a fiance's mother to a mother-in-law. It's too jolting.

A point of personal privilege is in order at this point. My own in-laws must not be read into every sentence of this chapter, especially my mother-in-law. We get along fine. We don't agree on everything that comes up, but we do share two major points of view. The first, both of us agree that she is James's mother. The second, we both agree I am his wife. James concurs in both opinions.

Now, we have never sat down to discuss either of these points, but early after the wedding we began gradually to agree on these two points which cause so many new daughters-in-law trouble.

An inestimably helpful factor in these relationships is James's decisiveness. He has never once given me any reason to feel that his mother would be allowed (should she try) to usurp my place and privilege as wife. I feel sure, at least I hope, that he never gave Mrs. Fancher any reason to feel that his growing love for me would lessen his love for her. He has never been forced, so far as I can tell, into a "me or your mother" situation. If he has, I'm unaware of it and sorry for it.

And don't get the idea that Mrs. Fancher and I have haloes and wings. We are both quite strong-willed and highly opinionated and sometimes just plain hardheaded, about like you and your mother-in-law. But we are Christian women and Christian principles work between two women, even when one is a daughter-in-law and the other a mother-in-law.

Here are ten suggestions for a daughter-in-law. A son-in-law could change just a few words and profit from them. They sound a little glib, but they don't mean to be.

One. Remember your husband's birth date. It was on that date when your husband became his mother's son forever. Children grow up for everyone but Mamma. Ever hear her treat your forty-year-old husband the same way you treat your three-year-old son? "Button your coat." "Where are your gloves?"

Most women never get over being a fellow's mamma. Really, there is no valid reason why they should.

Two. Remember she has feelings. At the risk of sounding highly trite I will set down the profound opinion that every good human relationship takes some doing.

Much as you might wish to, you can't relegate your mother-in-law to the crazy corner and dismiss her with, "She's just an old bat." She isn't.

She may be an old woman, but remember that the same aging process is at work on your raving beauty.

Three. Don't compete with her. Let her be his mother. You be his wife.

No need for both husband and wife to have to be pen pals to the mother-in-law. But let him write her—remind him to if you need to. Let him have interest in all their family's doing. You try to enjoy them, too. Be sure he remembers her birthday, Mother's Day, and any other day of special meaning, such as dates on which someone close died.

If there are family traditions which mean a lot to her, try to sustain them if agreeable to you and your husband. I have a thing about too much strong tradition which must be carried on no matter what. It puts people on an uncomfortable spot. Variation on holiday celebrations, for instance, makes it possible for a newly married couple to work out their plans without hurt feelings on either side. Many times a young bride goes along with a tradition because she would rather not incur the wrath of her in-laws by bucking tradition.

If his mother likes to make his favorite dish and bring it over, rejoice in it, so he can, too. Besides, it means less cooking. Count your blessings, girl.

Four. Start with her where she is. Not that you are going to take her anywhere. It is likely that less than a few of her attitudes are going to change. Unless she is a very young mother-in-law. Even then, percentages are still low.

Consider the number of times your own child has changed your mind about something and divide that by five (I don't know why I said five, any number will do). You will then have the approximate number of times you or your husband is likely to change your mother-in-law's mind.

Be perfectly honest with yourself and you may find that your mind would be better off to agree with her on some issues. Don't feel you have to disagree with her simply because she's your mother-in-law. That puts you in the back seat of the boat your teen-ager sits on the front seat of.

Five. Don't be so easily bugged. Before you have been around your mother-in-law three hours you will find some things about her that bug you. Most of them are not worthy of the attention you give them. Forget them, if you can. If you can't, try to find the humor in them.

My mother and my mother-in-law both will read this. At least, they'll never get another Mother's Day gift if they don't! This typical example of what I mean by the insignificant things that bug us includes both of them.

We drink iced tea the year around. I make it a gallon at the time and sweeten it when I make it. I know exactly how sweet my family likes it. That's how much I sweeten it.

For years when my mother came to eat she would make a face and ask if I forgot to sweeten the tea. For the same years when Mrs. Fancher came to eat she would make a face and say she didn't see how we could stand so much sugar.

I finally got to the place where I put the sugar bowl at Mother's place when she comes, and I make a separate pitcher of unsweetened tea for Mrs. Fancher's stay.

It embarrasses me that I let this bug me—and my whole family—for so long.

Six. Allow for individual differences of ability and intelligence as well as education, culture, experience. Remember that the scales will not tip in your favor in every area.

The fact that her ideas are different does not make hers wrong and yours right. Chances are that some of hers are right and some are wrong. The same chances apply to your ideas. Circumstances differ. Personalities differ, but some principles, like tolerance, acceptance, and respect, never differ. Don't let yourself be unable to learn.

Seven. Remember your birth date. Why? You were born a woman. The law of averages will probably make you a mother-in-law one of these days. The Golden Rule, you know.

Eight. Now, what do you do? After you have done all this, sift her through your tolerance sieve. Decide what you can put up with and what you can't.

You know what to do about what you can put up with. You put up with it. But the important thing is the manner in which you put up with it. If you aren't careful, putting-up-with will give birth to several very negative emotions. Like resentment, like disgust, like impatience, like jealousy, and maybe like several other ones, depending on your temperament.

It is not enough to tolerate. Toleration must not impose a sense of uneasiness in the mother-in-law, nor on your husband, nor on you.

Now, what to do about what you can't put up with.

Well, you can always seethe with some of these unlovely emotions we have been talking about. But that's no good. You need the understanding of your husband to be able to work around the things about his mother that bother you.

Talk about it with your husband but not in a tone of voice or with implications that his mother is a dud. He should love her, and part of his good behavior toward you comes directly from his love for her. Chances are that his merely knowing that something bothers you and that he is sympathetic with you about it will relieve much of the bother, possibly enough of it that you will need go no further with the matter.

However, if it is a matter that really does need to have something done about it, maybe both of you need to talk with her about it, if you're brave enough. This is risky, but growing hostility is even riskier. The important thing is that you do not damage anyone's self-respect. If an issue is important enough to be discussed, it is important enough to be settled with dignity. Discussion should result in understanding on both sides.

Let's take a for instance. Say the point of contention is the children's bedtime during a weeklong visit from grandparents. This seems to me to be a point at which a set of parents should decide. Ground rules for a home do not really need the attention of outsiders. The household goes along nicely for all the time the grandparents are not there, so parents should be allowed to fill their customary roles when a grandparent is present.

It may be necessary for a husband to say to his mother, "Mother, Sally really is a capable mother. I believe it would be less frustrating to her and to the children if you do not suggest what time they should or should not go to bed (or what TV they watch or should not watch, how they should dress or what they should be made to eat or what time they should be made to come in, etc., whatever the point in issue may be)."

Such a procedure may make the current visit slightly unsuccessful, but it may pave the way for much more successful visits in the future. Children feel tension from having to receive orders and suggestions from too many adults. Perhaps the lovely small child-grandparents relationships come to an end not because of the ages and change of interests of the children, but because of the way grandparents act too much like parents as the children get older. Most any teen-ager would agree that one set of parents is a gracious plenty.

Nine. Consider her typical week. In contrast to your week— busy, full, and rewarding—consider a typical week in her life. Remember, now we are thinking of homes where there are teenagers. This means many grandmothers will be older women, many of them widowed and living alone.

Look for the actual work she does (in or out of her home), such as club work, civic work, church work and attendance, times she gets together with friends, correspondence she receives and answers, visitors she has, hobbies she follows, times she visits your family, times she writes your family, times she calls your family.

Thus you can see how much of her time is actually touched by your family.

Then consider your week. Examine all the same things.

Here's what I'm driving at. Chances are pretty slim that you are in each other's hair as much as you think you are. At the same time, two kinds of contact are absolutely necessary if you live in the same town, three if you do not.

The first is visits. Something has to be worked out so that the mother of your husband and grandmother of his children is able to be in their physical presence. There is no substitute of any kind for this—visits are a must. How well you all get along with each other and the domestic situations will have to be the main indicators of frequency, length, and nature of these visits—yours at her house and hers at your house.

Getting this worked out early in marriage is another must. Privacy in the first months of marriage is an important factor, but occasionally older people forget and offer themselves for all kinds of help. If there is anything most just-marrieds (to say nothing of long-marrieds) do not want, it is help.

By "help" I mean interference in decisions, plans, and such. Our society is set up in such a way today that many parents do give financial help so that marriage may take place earlier and be easier. Whether this is right or wrong I will not try to say. I do think, though, that if financial help is given, the help should be simply the giving over of money, rent-free quarters, or whatever other form the help takes. It should stop there. No strings should be attached to its use and such. If the help can't be given trustfully with a sense that it will be used to help the couple keep themselves in the will of God and get ready to do whatever God wants them to do, perhaps the help should not be given at all. So much for one woman's opinion. Back to the subject that most young couples, as well as couples of all ages, do not really want outside "help" as defined above.

I remember the delicious feeling—because I still have it—that James and I could do anything we needed done. This sounds very excluding, doesn't it? That's part of the miracle of love. Married folks should be allowed complete privacy from the beginning.

At the beginning there are two opinions, his and hers, about everything that comes up. Many times these two opinions must be reconciled, compromised, or fused. Any third and fourth opinions only add to the confusion.

But this pipe-dream opinion of mind that privacy from the beginning is a must is an abstract. I have rarely seen it in the concrete. Advice to newlyweds is like advice to new mothers. Everybody has an easy, never-failing answer to questions they are not even asked.

Well, if opinions are given when they are not sought, it appears impossible for much privacy of mind and business, doesn't it? That's about what it is—impossible.

So, what's the point? Simple: keep your mouths shut about your business. For instance, if you are about to buy something, keep your mouth shut until you have bought it. If you need anyone's advice, seek it. My rule-of-thumb is that husband-and-wife-made decisions turn out best.

There is something about the shopping, thinking, talking, looking, and finally deciding that is thrilling for just two people to share. It is easier to go along with your husband's wishes if emotions don't get snarled up with divided loyalties—his or yours—to one or more parents.

The second kind of contact is phone calls. If you are in the same town, neither of you must become a nuisance to the other. If you are not in the same town, you must call occasionally to keep in voice touch.

The third kind of contact is letters. Work out a suitable plan for all. If she doesn't feel she has heard from her son if you write the letter, then by all means, have him write.

Ten. Look at your feet. They place you between her and her son, she probably feels. If her feelings are right, pick your feet up and get out from between them. A good mother deserves to feel joy and pride in her son's attentive love.

Now, suggestions to mothers-in-law.

One. Remember your son's wedding anniversary. It was on that date when your son became her husband forever, hopefully. She is now his first responsibility and should be allowed his first allegiance.

Two. Remember she has feelings. It is an intense time for her. She needs tenderness and kindness from every quarter. Not too much, though, just enough to show that you're human.

Three. Don't compete with her. Let her be his wife. You be his mother. She'll soon learn to take care of him well enough that he'll survive.

Four. Start with her where she is. She's just a child, at first, it seems. Gradually she grows into a fine, mature woman, quite capable of rearing your grandchildren. Though her rules may seem somewhat different from the ones you used to rear her good husband, close examination shows they're not too far away, after all.

If she wants your help in growing up herself or in helping rear the children, let her ask for it. She probably will if you don't beat her to the draw and start giving advice and help she hasn't asked for.

Five. Don't be so easily bugged. She will have her own way of doing things. Her family may be quite different from the way you'd like it to be. Try to let them live their own lives, and love them while they live them.

Six. Allow for individual differences and enjoy the newness it can bring into your life.

Seven. Remember your birth date. Why? It reminds you there's a generation's worth of time between you and her. And you know what that means—things are different, now.

Eight. At the point of what-do-you-do, the mother-in-law really has little choice but to stand back and let her son's family's world go on without suspicion, distrust, and disdain. Some big order, that's for sure.

If you feel you must put in some opinion or objection, create pleasant circumstances under which to do so. Remember, losing fellowship is a sad experience. Be sure the issue is worth it before you risk it.

And when you have expressed an opinion, don't nag. Don't mention it every time you are together. The fact that you expressed your opinion may not have changed their way of doing.

Nine. Remember your son's birth date. That when you became *his* mother, not *hers.* The traditional thought that mothers become community property in marriage is sweet in theory and may become true in practice if either partner did not have a mother prior to marriage. For the wife or husband who has been reared by a loving mother to be expected to bestow on someone else's mother the same loving esteem and affection she has for her own mother is beyond sound expectation, and the inability of a person to do so should not be looked upon by a mother-in-law as a sign of rejection.

There is no magic in the wedding ceremony that transforms any person involved, and the roles of the mothers will be filled by the same two who filled them before the children were joined in marriage. I do not agree with the last half of the old saying, "I did not lose a son, I gained a daughter."

My mother will always be my mother, but she will never be James's mother, no matter how much they love each other. But the same token, Mrs. Fancher will always be James's mother, and never mine.

Basically, the fallacious tradition of a mother's expecting to become overnight mother to her new in-law may cause more strife than any one other thing because assuming the place of mother means exercising the duties of motherhood, such as instructing, suggesting, ordering, and the like; it means infringing on rights that belong to the wife or husband; it means meddling in places that are none of her business; it means expressing opinions when they have not been asked for and usually are not needed.

Ten. Consider her typical week. Remember how busy yours was when your family was at the stage hers is now. Chances are she doesn't have as much domestic help as you had, though she surely has more conveniences. Be thoughtful of her energy. She scarcely has enough to go around.

Try to do things that will help her, not things that will add to her work. But you must learn what she considers help and what she feels is interference.

A daughter expects and wants things from her own mother that she does not want from her husband's mother. For instance, it has always been fine with me for Mother to help me clean my house when she comes and to mend clothes for us, or do any of the chores I haven't gotten done.

But I want to have the house already spotless before James's mother comes and would rather she didn't know I'm behind on the mending, or anything else. Silly, I guess. I must be working to convince myself there *is* such a thing as a perfect daughter-in-law, and that I'm it.

At least, we keep trying, don't we?

Her Budget

To parody a well-known poet, "More fusses are caused by money than this world dreams of."

That may not be exactly true, for most people do realize what a trouble spot this area of homelife can be. Without a doubt, it is one of the places where the whole family can get caught and find itself snarled and bound, sometimes almost hopelessly.

Several things ought to help a Christian woman in her attitude about her budget. Facetiously speaking, maybe the word itself is a challenge because of our sort of slang word "budge." A woman is likely to try to "budge" her money a little more and a little more until she has budged it too much, and there's trouble.

I have found all kinds of definitions for the word "budget." Some definitions make a budget very binding; others make it very loose. None of the definitions satisfy me, nor have I tried to come up with one of my own. We have tried practically every approach to the budget at our house. None we ever set up came out even with the money or with the month.

Seems to me if a budget can be looked on as a principle for using the family income to accomplish family purposes, it makes the whole business easier. But we'll explore that more fully a little later.

First, what should be a woman's attitude toward her family's money. Where should she get her attitude? From her mother? Her friend? Her husband?

How about from the Bible?

Maybe of all the attitudes a Christian woman brings to her new home none will have to be reshaped and reworked as will her ideas about money. Scarcely ever does a girl step from one financial situation to an identical one. More often than not she finds herself with a much lower income and a smaller and less convenient place to live.

If the responsibility of having to work as well as to keep house and to care for her new husband is added to the physical and emotional adjustments of marriage, a bride may feel snowed under before she begins.

This may, in itself, be the real point of conflict—before she begins. Maybe because it is so difficult for youngsters to accept teaching and advice from parents during late adolescent years, young people are not taught the management of money. It is much simpler not to argue with adolescents, so parents take the less stormy way too often.

This indicates that perhaps the time to teach management of money is during the years of a child's life when he does listen and learn from adults, not the teen-age years when simply the fact that one of his parents says a thing is white makes the teen-ager determined to see it as black. Beginning early is vital.

A small child is able to understand the sharing principle quite early—from the time he offers his mother a swig from his nippled bottle, and later, a lick off his sticky grape sucker.

He learns early that bartering is a way of life—when he is allowed to ride a playmate's pedal car in exchange for the playmate's being allowed to use his Play-Do factory. Children are often rather shrewd, wheeling-dealing horse traders.

Thus, from their everyday play, small children can bring perception to an explanation of family finances. A child misses an important part of his belonging to a family if he doesn't have any idea how the whole business goes on.

For many children money is a squabble item. It's what doesn't grow on trees. It's what parents don't have enough of. It's what children think their daddies are made of. It's what everything costs. it's what children shouldn't keep asking for. It's what children keep wheedling for and usually get.

For many others it is life's all-important item. It's what Daddy must work long hard hours to get. It's what must be come up with to keep up with whatever family is being kept up with. It's what Mother has to go to work to make so the family can have more of what it will buy.

Relatively few children grow up with a healthy attitude toward money. Even when parents have a healthy attitude themselves, too few take time to help the child develop a healthy one.

A child should hear an explanation of a family's financial set-up from time to time beyond the statement that he (or some other family member) either *cannot* have something or that he *can* have something. That is about as far as most families go, but there should be an easy explanation made to the child, showing him what the family has available to spend every month (or week or two weeks). He can understand that a check (or cash or money order) each month is what the family trades to a bank, loan company, or landlord for the right to live in a house, trailer, or apartment. He understands it in terms of swapping toys, games, turns.

In the same framework he can understand that his mother trades the grocer money for the family's food. All the way you can carry him and show him that occasionally (hopefully, only occasionally) there is not enough money left for all the trading that is absolutely necessary. When that happens the "extras" that would be nice will have to wait longer. He knows if he has two toy trucks to trade and three friends to trade trucks with that he just can't make a deal with the third without a problem. If your small child is bright enough you may even explain the pitfalls of trading beyond your safe ability to trade.

With this sort of understanding of financial set-up in the family, the child can grow into a mature and wise attitude toward money and what it can do and what it cannot do.

It isn't the purpose here to try to show ways to economize to stay within whatever budget principle a family decides upon. All sorts of excellent materials along these lines are available in secular magazines and books. Besides, most of us know better how to handle money than we show by what we do in handling it. Our purpose, rather, is to look squarely at money for what it is worth, to examine its value to a Christian home.

A woman's attitude toward a budget principle must emerge from a proper concept of material possessions as she looks at them in a Christian framework, beginning with God's ownership of everything—the earth, its fulness, its dwellers.

A Christian framework which might be explained in a very elementary way is this: God made the world. He made man. He allows man to use the world and all its contents. Man in his use of these contents has a direct responsibility to God in the wise use of them. Everything a Christian family does should have as its aim to fit into the will of God for the family's life, as reflected in his will for each individual in the family.

Money, then, is to be used to help carry out God's plan for the lives in the family. This brings us back to the woman's attitude toward money. While other women find their attitudes in such secular bases as selfishness, social mores, and other such places, the Christian woman finds her attitude about money in a thorough understanding of the principles of Christian stewardship as set forth in the Scriptures. If you do not have that, a conference with your pastor should help you on your way to finding it.

In each of the parables which Jesus used to teach stewardship principles there is a leading role and a supporting role. The leading role is God—he is always shown as the owner. The supporting role is man—he is always shown as the steward.

A woman becomes a steward when something has been entrusted to her. At this particular point we are thinking of the material things that have been entrusted to Christian women in general, to *you* in particular.

It seems that the owner in each parable expected the money

which was entrusted to the steward to bear some returns. It never was sufficient that the amount of money simply be preserved as it was until the next day of reckoning. Therefore, it does not seem unreasonable for us to believe that all that God has entrusted to us should be caused to bear returns for its owner.

Most economically happy families seem to think a budget is necessary. You may call it "planned spending" if it eases the pain a little. The entire family should help in planning to spend the money it has available. the needs of every member must be considered. Most important things have to be decided. Almost every time something will have to be left out that one or more members of the family will be a bit sad about, but we must always remember, there is next month.

Secular sources for budget planning seldom give a Christian proportion to tithes. The first item in the Christian budget should be a tithe—10 simple percent—given through the church. Families who are faithful in this find a sense of joy and achievement from such gifts that they do not get anywhere else. For, when they hear of baptisms resulting from the work of an agricultural mission in Argentina, they can feel a part of it and of all other mission work their denomination supports.

There is a key person in the home so far as tithing is concerned. That's right, the Christian woman's being willing to allow the other nine tenths to be enough for her and the family often makes the difference in a man's being willing to tithe. It's very difficult for a man to channel $100 a month through his church if his wife and children are yelling for a new second car, and the $100 tithe is the only money he could use for the monthly payment. It may not be a second car at your house, but it may be something else.

There is another item that most secular budget-planners make too small—gifts. A family's giving should go beyond duty gifts —wedding, graduation, birthday, and such. About the loveliest of all Christian graces, after gratitude, is generosity. Giving should be taught children, not lavish, expensive giving, but loving, thoughtful, helpful giving.

The family which includes generosity in its budget soon learns how to give less expensively and can make the budgeted amount reach more people. What sort of giving do I mean? An album for an elderly neighbor whose income doesn't have room for such a purchase, a couple of yards of material and a pattern for a teen-ager who can sew but has limited funds, paperbacks for sick people, little needs that a gift can fill.

You're afraid such gifts might be insulting? There is a Scripture verse which helps here. It says something about Christians abounding in love. I understand this verse better because of the garden my friend Doris had in 1968.

Abounding in vegetables is the way we will always remember her garden. It provided enough vegetables for her family and then provided for my family, for her sister's family, and for her mother's family, and for numberless others. I even shared, with her permission, some of what she gave me with others. Her garden abounded in vegetables.

This is the way I, as a Christian, ought to be—abounding in love. I am to have enough love for my family and then for my neighbor's family, and for her sister's family, and for her mother's family, and numberless others. Each of these may even share the love I give them with someone else. Thus I will abound in love, having enough love for everyone.

How do I give love? Is a cake baked for a sick friend enough? Is a visit to a sad, lonely friend enough? Is a letter of encouragement to a friend enough? Is a sack of usable clothing enough?

Yes, the cake is enough—if the sick one cannot help but see in my eyes, when I hand her the cake, this abounding love. And the visit is enough—if the sad friend cannot help but hear in my voice, as I talk, this abounding love. And the letter is enough—if the despondent one cannot help but read between my lines this abounding love. And the clothing is enough—if the wearer cannot help but feel in my touch, as I smooth the wrinkles to see the fit, this abounding love.

Without love the cake is flat no matter how good it tastes; without love the visit is a duty no matter how gay; without love the letter is a chore no matter how pretty; without love the clothes are a near-insult no matter how long they are worn. It is the abounding love that makes the difference. The cake, the visit, the letter, the gift—each is a spill-over of the abounding love to which Christ commanded me. When love abounds, I cannot miss what I give away of it.

It is sort of like the egg and the chicken, the old thing about which comes first. It is sort of hard to tell which came first when a Christian woman has included generosity in her budget and finds love there, too. There is no insult in a gift given in love.

Another item many secular budget-planners leave out is one I call "Occasional Luxuries and Frivolities." Every budget ought to be arranged to allow an occasional frivolity and an occasional luxury. I remember once seeing a small child being allowed by her father to select a rather trashy 59¢ toy watch from a rack in a grocery store. It was obvious that they were extremely poor. They even looked undernourished. I wondered at the father's wisdom in spending even that amount of money for a toy. But the little girl's delighted smile made the father smile. There is no telling how luxurious that little child felt with her purchase around her wrist. That watch may find itself in a keepsake box one of these days. Or she may pull the memory of it from her mind when she has become old.

Big folks need frivolity and luxury occasionally, too. Carried to an extreme this could be dangerous, but when every member of the family knows that life will have its little fine things, life somehow goes easier.

It is healthful for a man and wife to decide what it is that they want from the husband's job. Money alone isn't enough. If the husband can hold out his paycheck and look at it while his heart has a reasonable amount of contentment, that is good.

Then, a woman must understand what her husband's income will do and won't do. And it will help a heap if they decide together what it must do first.

It isn't always a woman's demands that make a man work too hard. Often it is his drive for success and its by-products, money being one of the most outstanding.

Handling money includes: earning it, planning how to spend it, spending it for what you planned, making yourself quit spending after that.

Sounds simple? It is. The secret is in being able to see these four principles of handling money in the light of Christian eternity.

Whatever a Christian does to earn money must be completely honorable. It must not be involved with any product or business that is detrimental to human character. His behavior in earning it must be Christian.

Planning how to spend it includes being able to see your Christian goals as attainable and using your money to attain them. For instance, most every woman wants as nice a house to put her home in as she can possibly have. Many women have set their sights so high on housing that finanacial disaster resulted. For others financial disaster did not result, but ulcers for a husband under pressure resulted—homes have broken, you've heard the whole bit. Plan your housing, along with all the other necessities in your budget, within your reach so that a house will not be all you have left when the home gets so unhappy. That's just one example. Keep in mind, too, that your reach is likely to get longer some time in the future.

The essentials for living come in much nicer packages than they used to. Thus they cost more. We have let advertising snow us under. Everything advertising says is essential just isn't. How do you decide what is essential for your family? You don't. You let the family help to decide.

Talk, talk, talk, but don't argue. Talking helps you decide how you really think about something you have wanted. It helps you whip your sense of values into shape. Hearing another point of view may take some of the edge off your point of view. Come to grips with what the money you have available should do to help all your family stay within the will of God. It is often surprising to find out how cooperative children can be when they understand why they are being cooperative.

After the money is earned and its spending is planned, the problem of staying within the plans shows up. Sometimes it may seem impossible to get along without some item you see and want with all your heart, but is not in your spending plans for this week. Discipline is the word. Also, think back to some items you felt the same way about in the past and see if they remained as important *after* you bought them. Most of mine didn't. This helps me a great deal nowadays when I'm shopping.

There are things we need. Then there are things we want. Telling them apart is something else. The little buys are often the culprits in unbalancing our planned spending.

It is necessary to live with the idea in mind that there will always be a need to hold the reins so far as money is concerned. There just is no other way. Even as income increases, this remains necessary. Every week the planned spending must be examined.

Be honest about your finances. "Po'mouthing" is about as unbecoming a habit as a Christian can have. It is indicative of ingratitude for the blessings we do have if we grumble about something we don't have.

Honesty about finances includes another very important thing. It is dishonest to buy things you know you cannot pay for. It is dishonest, when you are already in debt and cannot keep up with your current bills and payments, to make additional purchases. Every penny should be used to clear the old debts away and thus clear the testimony you bear as a Christian. This is where the fourth principle—quit spending—comes in. Observing it frees one from the embarrassment of letters, phone calls, personal visits from people to whom money is owed for things that should never have been bought in the first place.

For the Christian woman, then, a budget is never an end. It is a means by which she keeps the vineyard entrusted to her in tip-top shape. Why keep it in such good shape? To produce the best fruit the branches of the Vine who live at her house can produce.

Using money to keep up with God's standards for us instead of our neighbor's standards is where the joy of stewardship comes in. Then it makes sense to shop the sales, buy the cheaper cut of meat most of the time, cut down on car costs—all the things that make money go further and accomplish more for the people who are using it.

There's no perfect budget, but the Christian woman whose joy is in the Lord is willing to keep trying to find one.

She knows one day her joy will be completely full when this parable she has the supporting role in is translated into an accounting of the returns which her talents have brought to the Owner.

Her Husband

Setting out with a husband toward hopefully the most fun part of life generates in the heart of a woman the best of emotions. It sparkles jewel-like fantasies into her head. It backs breath up into her throat with delight. It conjures myriad mirages of magic.

The road ahead is paved with marble instead of concrete, and the clouds are piles of whipped-cream dreams instead of rain-holders. The moon is less than a mile away, and the two of them will reach it with heart-propelled power in a journey of short duration.

She does not doubt it for a moment.

At first.

Then, occasionally she raises an umbrella and peeps out from under it disbelievingly at that cloud in the sky whose tears roll off the umbrella and splatter her feet. A few of her tears mix with them. She blinks her eyes at the road she's on. Marble would shed water better than this.

Then the cloud cheers up, the marble sheds the water, and her doubts are gone. Because love is growing, hearts are knitting together, and life is taking shape. Reality is emerging. For two who will to work at it, reality become the enchanted.

Loving each other on a holiday weekend is a cinch. There has been something enchanting to me when James and I have sat together in disappointment, crisis, even danger, and I have been able, at all the rainstops on the marble road, to look at him with faith unlimited and love unbelievable and know that we get closer to our moon every day.

Recently I was given an assignment at a writer's conference to write on "The Things I Like Most About My Home." Here is what I wrote.:

At home I am treated like a queen. The scepter in my hand is, in turn, a broom, a mop, or a spoon for stirring up a cake. Hanging in my closet, the regal robes resemble skirts and sweaters, dresses and coats. When I look in my bucket I see bubbles. The bubbles are not from champagne, but from suds for mopping with.

Numbering three, the royal subjects in my domain—Sir Bobby, Sir Frank, and Sir James Neil—pay me such homage as: "That cake was something else." "Thanks for washing my sweater," and, fairly often, "I love my mom."

Our king is a bald-headed one with abounding love and a marvelously good humor. He set the jewels b-e-l-o-v-e-d into a crown. Then he and the boys placed it on my head.

Nobody sees it but me, though. Everywhere else I am just a woman, a teacher, the preacher's wife, a customer, a driver, a pedestrian. But when I go into my home a transformation happens.

When I was a little girl, I dreamed about becoming a princess, and here I am a queen!

This is what real love is all about—making the one you love feel so very special.

There is no magic in the wedding vows. Everybody is the same, but everybody must begin to change. A son must change into a husband first. He remains a son second. A daughter must change into a wife. She remains a daughter second. All others suddenly become in-laws.

It was the quite-clear suggestion of Jesus that marriage was not to be dealt with in any manner that would cause the marriage to be torn asunder. Many, many "tears asunder" begin with tiny, tiny weak places which gradually get larger until the ripping sound is heard, and the ugly place shows.

A definite effort should be made by husband and wife from the beginning to find the weak spots which could eventually tear their marriage asunder. These should be strengthened against such possibilities.

It is rarely ever easy to admit weaknesses and correct the fault behind them, but beyond the civil legality of marriage, a husband and wife in a Christian home find their union blessed by the control of God's laws.

Some facetious individual has said that a cardinal rule for good marriage is that each partner gives 60 percent and takes 40 percent. Yes, sir, both have to give and take for a marriage to shape up.

Take Wesson Oil, for instance. You'll have to take Wesson Oil (not by mouth—take it, for example). I can't very often. There's a perfectly good reason. His name is James.

At our house we have taken togetherness pretty far—would you believe we often go grocery shopping together? But when it's time to buy cooking oil, I try to get away alone.

Something about shortening and cooking oil puts red dollar marks over James's retina. When he sees me pick up a container of Wesson Oil, he immediately speaks. I hear a commentary comparing the price of Risktex or Sleetdrift and other shortenings. All of them are reliable (and usually cheaper), and I'm sure each has a hallowed spot in the kitchens of a million or so women; rightly so.

But I am a Wesson Oil cook. Like I'm a Tide washerwoman. No matter what I buy this week, I come back to Tide and Wesson Oil next week. *If* I go to the grocery alone.

It's real funny—many of the bags of groceries James buys alone have a jar of cooking oil or a can of shortening—always a new kind. I think it is some sort of brainwashing process by which he hopes to diminish my exalted opinion of Wesson Oil. He thinks he'll finally wear me down.

What do I do with his purchases? Use them without a word. Then buy Wesson Oil every chance I get.

Some days the chicken is especially good. He says, "What did you fry it in?"

I say in a very controlled voice, in an unconcerned manner, "Wesson Oil." He has little say. Because he is not convinced. His next bag of groceries is likely to have a jar of Korny Oil in it.

What's the point of the Wesson Oil wrangle at our house? What point can it be stretched to prove? For my money (No, not mine; for James's money, the money he saves on Korny Oil), it's a classic example of the give-and-take that is necessary for good marriage.

It also says something for the possibility of civilized disagreement. Some might call it a cold war, but it isn't. It's really very warm—this feeling I have about our Wesson Oil dilemma. Both of us get our way part of the time, and it's surely better than the yell-and-tell method. He doesn't yell-and-tell me I am extravagant and stubborn (though I am about Wesson Oil). I don't yell-and-tell him he is stubborn and narrow-minded (though he is about Wesson Oil).

It's a sort of unstated policy of tolerance-without-fear. I'm not afraid to buy Wesson Oil. He's not afraid to bring home Korny Oil.

Civilized disagreement is necessary for happy marriage.

So is discipline necessary for marriage to be happy. For each marriage discipline has specific characteristics; its character conforms to the needs of the marriage. Good marriage demands the security resultant from physical fidelity, mutual dependence, and mental fidelity. Each of these requires discipline. Because discipline cannot sustain itself, it must have the best of both husband and wife.

The main discipline a Christian woman must exercise is to be sure she relates properly to her husband. She is the only wife he has, and she should want to keep it that way.

Look at your husband and decide what *he* needs from you today, this week, this month, this year. It may be as simple as a time of lovemaking; it may be as simple as cutting down the grocery bill (simple?); it may be as complicated as helping restore his confidence; it may be as demanding as helping him face a career crisis.

Most of us women say to ourselves on any given day something like, Well, today I have to wash, wax floors, finish Suzie's dress, make Johnny's cookies, finish my Sunday School lesson, write Mother, on and on, scarcely ever including the husband in a specific way in our plans. True, all our plans affect and include him, but he deserves something special all along.

It seems from what I've read and heard, that most married women eventually come to the place that they feel there has to be "something besides this." "This" meaning "just a husband, family, home." Nobody can give this feeling either a name or a definition. It is not consistent in the age group which it strikes. It just seems to strike after a woman has acquired those two prized possessions —a husband and some children. At least, she had anticipated they would be prized possessions. Maybe the rub came when they turned out to be human beings and she took the blue ribbons off them.

If a husband is a prize when he's caught, chances are he will remain a prize, *if.* If the same tactics that were used to catch him are employed to keep him. He'll respond to the same results of good grooming he responded to in the premarriage era. He'll respond to the same thoughtfulness, the same smile, the same sweet words.

Familiarity may or may not breed contempt, but it surely does breed sloppiness. Don't run around at home looking like a wife— look like a sweetheart, the prettiest you can.

Looking forward to marriage and a family made adolescence a more enjoyable time for most of us. The glow ought to last, even if it is slightly dimmed by the "dirty work" that we were not quite aware existed in the fine print of the marriage license and the birth certificates.

Looking forward to the days without the children should make us enjoy the days with the children much more. Before you heat the tar and pluck the feathers, be assured that I do not have the door open to push mine out and be assured that I enjoy my children (except the unenjoyable parts—like their stubborn streaks, their fussing, etc.). But I have no fear of being left alone in the house with James in a few years. Nor can I understand the loneliness for their children that makes husband and wife dissatisfied and bored with each other. Besides, I'll be disappointed if our boys do not find for themselves the happy life we enjoy.

Maybe one of the things a husband and wife had best practice from the beginning of marriage is contentment with each other. Maybe that's one of the things they should save for their old age—the ability to get along with and to be considerate of one another.

After the children are gone, the couple should not find itself "right back where they started." They should find themselves more aware of each other, more content with each other, more complementary to each other, more delighted with each other—in short, more in love with each other.

Husband and wife should have behaved themselves all the child-rearing years in such a way that they can delight in the child's growing up and being able to function as an individual, finding themselves able to delight in each other now that they're alone again.

Keeping up with each other is important. A couple may go along for years being busy and busier and busiest, not communicating sufficiently to see if they're still in tune the same as they were. Suddenly, at some point, they stop short, horrified to be so far apart.

Being honest is vital. It is a wise husband who recognizes danger signals in his wife's words, "It doesn't matter." Sometime it really does not matter, but this observation often covers a deep feeling that it really does matter but the wife doesn't intend to put herself in a position to have to show that something matters.

Several things may have led the wife to the use of this phrase. It may be that she has often expressed how she really did feel about something and it made no difference in the final decision. She feels if her opinion has no influence she will not express herself verbally and be dealt another blow to her pride, to say nothing of her heart.

Again, it may be that she already knows how her husband feels and does not wish to disagree with him. Maybe he doesn't allow disagreement with him very graciously.

Being aware that people change helps a couple grow older gracefully. One day James picked up one of my hands to kiss it. In astonishment he said, "Honey, your hand is beginning to look old," as if it could not possibly happen to me. I said—calmly, because I had already recognized the awful truth—"After all, it was on me when I was born and you know when that was."

A woman doesn't have to put aside charm and loveliness as the years rack up. *Youthful* charm and loveliness have to be left behind, and the woman who can leave youth behind—with its styles and fads—is a happier woman, for sure.

None of us likes to own the wrinkles and the gray hairs and the pounds that are harder to shed, but for every age there are becoming methods of good grooming, for charm and loveliness. There are becoming clothes styles and hair styles. There are becoming health activities for every age.

Don't ever quit being a womanly woman just because you aren't as young as you were twenty years ago. He isn't either, you know, but you like him just as well—hopefully, better. He deserves you to keep being attractive and exciting as the years go by. I don't know about you, but I kind of like to have my fair share of the admiring glances my husband has for nice-looking women!

Keep having fun with each other alone. Can't afford it? You may not can afford it, but I believe you can afford it a heap cheaper than you cannot afford it, especially if you can translate dollars into memories to grow old by.

The same pure pleasure a couple has in each other's company at the time of their marriage should be cherished and nourished, even after the children are on their way, small, when they're teenagers, and after they leave the nest. How? By a hurried trip to a movie, an elegant night out, an afternoon picnic and fishing, a quiet weekend in a near or distant city, even a long vacation alone.

A couple ought to be lovers, but they ought to be friends, too. It takes dogged persistence to keep any kind of friendship going. This is true of a friendship in marriage. Time together alone is necessary.

What to do with the children when you get away? Grandparents, if agreeable with all. I remember the first time that my parents took our oldest child home with them. He was six months old, and they were the most delighted folks you ever saw. And a good time was had by all.

Another possibility is friends whose children you can keep next month—parent pools, we could call them.

Professional homemakers are available if you can afford them.

What will this do to your children—this going off and leaving them or sending them somewhere else? Depends on the children, of course, but for the reasonably well-adjusted and secure child, a new experience should be broadening. They should be able to see the things their parents plan for them "just for fun" and then to see that adults like to do things "just for fun." They need to know "old folks" can have fun, especially together. Their appetites for the adult part of homelife need to be whetted. Fear and bewilderment, coupled with boredom and blah-ness, should not be a part of a child's concept of parenthood.

Husbands and wives ought to enjoy the children together. Such enjoyment means a rather high percentage of agreement between the parents about all the things that involve children. It also means acceptance of the qualities of each parent that show up in each child. A mother must deal with the quality in both husband and child.

A lot of husbands nowadays find joy in sharing in all the aspects of keeping a house for a family. Probably how much a man helps around the house depends more on his own assessment of his masculinity than on any other one thing. He does not feel required to find his virility in playing a traditionally virile role that removes a man from all responsibility at home and places that responsibility on the shoulders of the woman alone.

I believe it is a happy man who feels he places no jeopardy at all on the image of his manliness when he escorts his wife to the kitchen to help her get breakfast on the table—or anywhere else to help her do anything else necessary to keep the house going well and her shoulders a little freer from the heavy load.

My husband was the first grandson on the Parkes side of the family. His Grandmother Parkes, whom we called "Mamma Annie," thought he was something pretty special—she petted him and nearly ruined him, to be quite honest.

It was an interesting experience when James and I took our first child for his first visit to Mamma Annie's. Everything went great until time came for a diaper change. Mamma Annie was appalled to see James happily change that diaper. James explained that he helped with all the care of the baby—that when it was time for a night feeding he changed the baby while I prepared the bottle and that, sometimes, he even gave the bottle to the baby.

I had the feeling Mamma Annie never did forgive me for having made a sissy out of her James. But I really didn't. Not one ounce of his masculinity had diminished in those weeks since Bobby's birth. Nor has it at any time during all the help he has given me with all three of the boys.

He likes to say that I taught them to call me "Daddy" during the day, so they'd call for "Daddy" at night, and he'd get up with them. I didn't, because he never needed any prompting, and their spirits are keenly perceptive of his love for them as evidenced in his sharing the care taken of them.

A husband and a wife each find their joy together in the children, but this should never take the place of the joy they have first in each other. Love for and enjoyment of children is no substitute for love for and enjoyment of each other.

How about jealousy in marriage?

It is sort of normal. It should be under control, of course. Women are jealous of all sorts of things—some of them are tangible, some of them are not. One woman is made jealous by something which would not make her neighbor bat an eye.

Husbands and wives should know what makes their mate jealous and avoid it like the plague. The contest is over when a couple gets married. While a little intentionally provoked jealousy may be good during courtship, it has no place in marriage.

Just as no one can predict what will make a person jealous, neither can anyone say the best way to treat jealousy when it comes. One woman reacts favorably to one treatment of jealously which would infuriate her neighbor. Manifestations of, reaction to, and treatment of jealousy must be dealt with every time they come up.

Jealousy really should be avoided, if at all possible. Watch suspicions. Don't let imagination feed them. Have confidence in yourself as a mate, and you'll have more confidence in him. Oftentimes it is doubt of ourselves that causes us to doubt others. There's a psychiatric term "projection" which means something like this—a person attributes his own unconscious drives and desires to others.

It is a sad commentary on Christian adulthood that many Christian couples have to deal with the fact and consequence of adultery. I have always felt that a man worth all the worry of catching is worth keeping. Expend the same energy and wiles to keep him that would be used on a partner in adultery, and you will find that he'll be giving you the same admiring glances, consideration and gifts he would to a partner in adultery. Adultery for the Christian is wrong, makes no difference what the provocation.

The double standard we hear so much about is wrong, too. It is just as important that a man keep the faith in marriage as it is that a woman keep it. I'll even be old-fashioned enough to venture my strong opinion that I think it is just as right for a single man to refrain from sexual relations as it is for a single woman.

A husband at some time sets his financial goals for life and heads toward them. They may be as simple as providing a good, plain living for his family with each child finishing high school. They may be as demanding as becoming a millionaire. Whatever they are, they seem too often to be his reason for living.

A healthy thing for a woman to do early in her husband's career is to try to get him interested in a good many things besides his economic goals. Remembering that a Christian home exists as a tool for spreading Christianity, a wife should help her husband find joy in religious work. This is a means by which the husband may lose sight of too high and too ambitious goals, or it may be the means by which his total concept of money and ambition are brought into line with Christian stewardship.

A wife must not be too anxious to get a lot of material things. This adds to her husband's drive to succeed so that he can satisfy her desires for more and nicer things. A wife who disciplines herself to find joy in things that cost less is one of the best insurances against ulcers that a husband can have.

Nothing is so dismal as a husband's feeling of failure. It brings him agony. It casts a pall over everything. It is the task of the wife to comfort him and help him see before today and beyond today.

The time may come when he feels he can never reach the goals he has dreamed of. This he calls failure. It is the responsibility of the wife to help him take inventory and see that today is good.

If a goal which means a lot to your husband has been missed and is now recognized as unattainable, what does a Christian woman do? You reassure him of the traits which make you love him. And you shouldn't have to try to think of them when the time comes. You should be honest with yourself at all times about all the good that is in your husband.

You let him know that your love does not depend on his accomplishments, that your respect is as great as ever.

There are usually advantages to any seemingly disadvantageous situation. Search them out and use them to advantage.

The distasteful part of failure is that it usually requires some adjustments, often very difficult ones. The Christian woman is the one who leads the way to the adjustments. You must be the proverbial tower of strength for your husband and family. Your attitude will do more than anything else to make the experience endurable.

Whatever has to be done to relieve the tension caused by your husband's failure—or his feeling of failure—you must dig in and do it. Be sure that you do not give him reason to feel worse.

He's not perfect, either, but with the right encouragement and your abiding love, he'll soon be trying again. There's nearly always tomorrow.

While failure creates chaos, success is not always easy to live with. Its taste may drive him on harder than ever. Its monetary rewards may cause the family some problems. There seem to be many families who can not learn to get along *with* money nearly as well as they can *without* it. I have had some rich friends who were very sad people.

Success, like everything else involving a Christian family, finds its worth in making the Christian life more meaningful in terms of personal involvement in actual Christian activity.

Such should be the reaction of a Christian woman to her husband's success—the fruits of it in satisfaction, contentment, and financial security should cause her whole household to be better Christians. If it does not, the family should sit down together and see why it doesn't.

There are some guidelines for good marriage that I do not think need any elaboration, but they do need to be put in this chapter somewhere. So, I decided to put them here before I get to that subject all America is intrigued with—sex.

Keep able to feel wonder. Don't let feeling get drab.

Express appreciation to your husband. Let other folks know about the nice things he does—not offensively, of course.

Get genuinely interested in some little something outside yourselves, but save some of your energy for yourselves together.

Look at yourself and give the gifts you have to give. Love can't work a miracle unless it is received.

Locate the fun in your man. Discover all the facets of his personality. Don't be so prim that you cause him to repress himself. Enjoy having him around, even to muddy shoes through the kitchen and his ties on doorknobs.

Keep your quarrels aimed away from yourselves. Stick to the subject being quarreled about. Don't refer to old quarrels. Stay in the present. Having happy sex after a quarrel is fine, but do try to get around to solving the problem which caused the quarrel.

Keep physically close to your husband.

Don't settle down with boredom. Fight against stodginess.

Dismantle your differences as carefully as if they were a bomb which could explode in your faces. They can do just that.

Now, to sex. I'm glad I got here before sex. No, I'm not confused. Yes, I know where babies come from.

But I'm glad I got here before practically everybody bought the idea that sex is a product. I'm glad that during my teen-age years it was still fine for a girl to decide that her virtue and chastity were worthy of being kept for Mr. Right.

I think it is still fine for a girl to be virtuous and chaste, but I'm told I'm in the minority. If this be true, this is a case where the majority is wrong.

I'll leave the how, when, and where to those who write more scholarly and technological books, but I am about to explore the why of sex.

Why should a couple work to achieve a good sex life?

1. It's fun. No marriage counselor should use mournful, dull tones about sex. The books given young folks to read should involve spiritual implications of sex, the excitement, the beauty of it all, not just mechanics.

2. It's for marriage. Boy, how Victorian can you get? I used to think maybe we were a little strict about this, but, you know, I've lived long enough to see that the happiest marriages are those whose partners have fit sex into the Christian framework of mar-

riage. Its enjoyment has helped their lives to be full, rich, and faithful.

3. It's fun. A lovely way to say, "I love you."

4. It's dangerous. A couple doesn't just find itself sexually adjusted or fulfilled. Each must come to marriage with a desire to have a good sex life, and then work at it.

The old joke that it is mighty pleasant work is not necessarily so. Many couples have a difficult time with sexual adjustment because they come to marriage without a real understanding of what sex is and what it is for and how to go about it for the right purposes. Therefore, sex is dangerous. It needs clarification.

Like I said, I don't intend to write a manual of Christian sex at this point. There have been some good books written on the subject. Get your pastor or counselor to tell you the titles of some of these, read them, and use whatever good you find there for your particular need. Don't let them make slaves of you, of course, but you'll find help. Steer clear of the sensational secularly popular books about sex. Many of them fail to have any presentation of the spiritual implications of sex. Most of them fail to put sex in the framework of marriage, too.

5. It's fun, and nearly always different. Variety is the spice of life, but it should be with each other, only.

6. It is thrilling and clean. Sex doesn't need a fence of dirty humor and distrust built around it. Rather, it needs a healthy attitude toward it which shows itself in a subdued and quiet manner toward the subject when sex is considered in light of a real-live relationship.

7. It's fun. But it's fun only when two people use it properly to enhance their love for each other, to give pleasure to each other, and to accent their complete belonging to each other. It is quite special when it's kept between just two people.

What are some of the greatest dangers to a happy sex life? Fatigue, selfishness, misunderstanding about sex, lack of privacy, unsettled disagreements, on and on we could go with the things that affect good husband-wife relationships. Whatever the difficulty or danger, its working out is well worth it.

We have a lovely analogy of the husband-wife relationship in *all* of marriage in the New Testament: Husbands love your wives even as Christ loved the church and gave himself for it. Wives submit yourselves unto your husbands.

What woman wouldn't find joy in being submissive and subordinate to a husband whose love would allow him to die for her?

There's no perfect husband-wife relationship, but this gets close.

Her Children

If all babies could get here wanted and loved, that would be great. Because too many of them don't, their parents have double trouble—maybe even triple trouble: physical care of a child, wrestling with their emotions about the child, and probably tussling with their muddled-up feelings toward each other in light of the child's presence and demands.

So, perhaps the first thing to consider in a chapter on children is the fact that a couple need not increase the size of the family until they want to. This book has no medical or sociological purposes except as medical or sociological facts are involved in working the Christian principles that make for happy homes. Such a medical fact is the availability of safe, convenient, inexpensive methods of birth control.

It's as simple as a statement: "Doctor, we really would like to wait about having a child. I'm sure you can suggest a safe method for us to use," and following properly the doctor's suggestions.

This advice would seem very elementary and unnecessary until we consider the astonishing number of babies being delivered to parents who did not wish to have them, to say nothing of the illegitimate births and abortions in our country each year. I did not search for any statistics on these numbers. We read them all along, and they increase with every printing. Furthermore, each of us can look around among the people we know and see that such occurrences are in far too high a percentage.

Planned or unplanned, children do keep coming. One day James was in a home where the youngest child was an adorable brunette boy, a real lively one. The child's father, after some typical behavior on the boy's part, said, "Boy, what am I going to do with you?"

He got a quick reply, "Keep me and feed me."

This just may summarize the responsibility parents have toward their children. It is the way that these responsibilities are met that make the difference.

A child's body houses two, I think—an imp and an angel. Mothers must deal with both and be sure not to let either one run rampant. I'm not sure how many a mother's body houses. I think most of the time there is only one in residence in me and it is no angel.

Everybody but mothers says what a mother's duty is. She would have to be an angel to live up to the gorgeous image of motherhood.

Neither does it follow that the inability of mothers to live up to their images is what's wrong with the world. A mother may try all day and half the night to teach her child to consider other people; she may set a lovely example for him. Yet, he may be the least considerate kid in town. I've seen this happen, haven't you?

If a mother were the only influence on her child she could take all the blame, or praise, as the case may be. But everything else is an influence on the child.

One mistake with your child may have an effect on him but it won't maim him for life or bring the world to an end.

Nobody has yet come up with an explanation of the quirk of a woman's psyche which causes her to expect from her children something which she herself cannot give—that ideal that we scratched at the outset of this book, perfection.

A baby is a baby. A child is a child. An adolescent is an adolescent. A young adult is a young adult. A middle-ager is a middle-ager. An old person is an old person. How are those for profound, earth-shaking statements? But, you know, it is such simple premises as those that a woman tucks away in her store of knowledge and does not pull out often enough.

I think I would be a much better mother if I knew my house

were bugged and I would be required to listen—every night—to every word I had said that day. It seems that knowing my children are naturally bugged and will hear over and over again every word I say would have more bearing on me than it does. Reckon what that says to me about myself? I try not to listen to what it says, I'm afraid.

Anyway, if my house were bugged and I did have to listen to me every night, I am sure one of the most repeated words would be, "Now, you ought to know better than that." And the emotions I'd hear in it would be disgusting.

It really isn't fair for us mothers to anticipate behavior beyond the wisdom of whatever age our child is. Assuming upon their store of knowledge is a mistake. It is a grueling task—this teaching children. Then it is a grueling task, to them, to practice what they have learned.

Children must be taught, but they have to learn for themselves, too.

When I was a little girl, I called an uncle of mine "Howdy Brown" (his name was Howard Brown), and I called my aunt "Big Tinky." They called me "Little Tinky." You may correctly gather from these terms of affection that I was always tickled to get to visit them in Memphis.

Their neighbor had a niece, Ada Jo, about my age, eight at the time of this tale, and we had fun together. Big Tinky's thumb was rather green and among her pretty flowers was one she called an "ice plant."

Stupid questions got stupid answers then, too, so when I asked Howdy Brown why it was called an ice plant, he told me, "Because if you touch it, you'll turn into ice."

Boy, talk about intrigue. Ada Jo and I were drawn to that plant and all its possibilities like Casey Stengel to Yankee Stadium. We stood looking at it for minutes at a time, fascinated and fearful, discussing the credibility of Howdy Brown's answer.

Both of us were pretty bright, and pooling our wisdom, we knew he had to be joking, but he never backed down from his warning that we would turn into ice the second we put a finger to the plant.

The number of days this went on I can't remember, but I know it was several. One more afternoon we again failed to get Howdy Brown to admit he was joking, so we told him and Big Tinky that we were going to touch it and see. Begging us not to do this, they went into the house.

Our curiosities had stood the strain as long as they could. We agreed we would both touch the plant at exactly the same time so if one froze, she would have the frozen company of the other. Deep breaths were taken several times before we finally met one another's eyes with a nod of our heads, and we slowly reached our hands out.

Just as we made contact with the plant, already feeling chilling up our spines, we heard loud delighted laughs just inside the window by which we were standing. Howdy Brown and Big Tinky knew we just had to learn for ourselves, and they had gone inside to watch our bravery. They were howling with delight about it.

We felt like howling, too, but not from delight.

It wasn't funny to us. We thought, for sure, that the sudden sound of laughter was an ice god somewhere in an ice heaven shrieking gleefully over his two new ice children who were about to be born by touching the ice plant. Relief was sweet when we realized we were still warm and soft, not cold and hard. We had finally found out.

Any young folks who may have struggled through this far in the book, let me remind you that the credibility of adults is not the point here. The determination of children to prove or disprove almost anything that comes up is the point.

If Howdy Brown had been right, we would have turned to ice. Possibly we would have melted by now, but whether we'd still be puddles of water or have evaporated, I don't know. We just aimed to find out for ourselves if we'd turn into ice.

Unfortunately, too many proofs children feel compelled to make do not have the happy ending ours did. Sometimes you do turn to ice, figuratively. Occasionally, turning into real ice might beat what does happen.

A child needs someone to teach him the things he needs to know. He must have faith and trust in the person so that he can know when the person tells him something, it is true. So many experiences of learning carry with them dire consequences—like a young person who must prove or disprove the effects of drugs. If young people can have a deep trust in enough adults they know personally to believe those adults when they say that drugs are harmful, maybe they can be in a better position to resist proving it for themselves.

It is towards such a trust that a mother begins when she first tells her toddler that a stove is hot.

Back to the statement that a child should know better. He shouldn't know better unless someone has tried to help him learn. Sometimes we parents chicken out. I did, not long ago.

The news analyst was discussing gonorrhea. I thought, Yep, James Neil (then twelve) will ask me any time now.

And he did, "What's gonorrhea?"

Because I had heard that parents should give short, concise, nonelaborated answers, I gave one.

"A venereal disease."

That's all I said, and then I held my breath for the next one.

James Neil rather sarcastically said, "You know I know what that is, don't you?"

My mouth flew open and my tongue hung limp waiting for my brain to send words. But James Neil walked off as if he couldn't care less about not getting an answer.

I loaded the dishwasher but never did come up with an answer to take to his room where he was studying. If he were a better speller than he is, I would figure he looked it up in a dictionary. Since he isn't, I'm hoping he forgot the whole thing. But I know what the chances of that are. If he really pursued it, there's no telling what definition he got from his playground buddies. But I deliberately and hurriedly chickened out.

This was a rather extreme set of circumstances, but there are countless times when parents chicken out at teaching something their children need to know. My children must have answers to questions I didn't even have to ask.

Childhood is a mighty important time. I'm still trying, but I'm undecided on how I feel about psychiatry in general; however, one of the suggestions of psychiatry that I do sort of go along with is the importance placed on childhood experiences, specifically a child's relationship with parents.

For instance, something occurred to me on our last trip to Disneyland. Disneyland, of course, is supposed to be about the most-fun place in the world, especially for children. It seems it would follow that it would be a most-fun place for parents, too, when they see their children have a delightful time. I do believe, though, that I saw more unhappy children and parents, per capita, that day then any other one day in my life. Parents yelled at children, yanked them by the arm and dragged them along, spanked them, and I even saw a few slappings.

What kind of memories can children have of Disneyland if they're treated like that? True, some of them were not on their best behavior—each exhibited some of the characteristics of a child whose excitement about such a trip had built up over days and days, perhaps even weeks. They were keyed-up, shrill-voiced, hungry, impatient, nervous, thirsty, hot, irritable, thoroughly childish. Isn't childishness a child's prerogative?

I thought how like that Disneyland trip many childhoods are. How can a child enjoy childhood if he is going to be yelled at, yanked up and dragged through it, and hit on occasionally? Not much, wouldn't you say?

Childhood deserves gentleness. Firm gentleness, but gentleness.

One reason childhood deserves gentleness is that in a few brief years adolescence hits a child smack in the face—suddenly he needs to know who he is—not John Doe generalization, but real personal recognition. He needs to know how to become independently related to his parents and his world. He needs to know what to do with these strange new physical feelings he's having, these new emotions he feels. He thinks of a new question every day.

He needs to find the answers to all of these in a Christian framework in which people live with purpose to life, followed by purpose to death. It should not be too difficult for a teen-ager to understand life by seeing himself as one of God's created beings, procreated by his parents, here on earth to help make the world Christian. In the same way he should be able to see death as the conduit through which a Christian goes from eternal spiritual life hampered by the temporary and the physical to eternal spiritual life unhampered by anything, from the eternal presence of God intruded upon by the presence of Satan to the eternal presence of God unhampered by any evil force.

For help in finding some of these answers, adolescents need communication with their parents, civil communication. They need the kind of communication in which children are not made to feel they're stupid and parents are not made to feel ignorant. About the only way the latter happens is for a parent to steel himself, grit his teeth, and wait to speak until he has firmly in mind that he is an adult dealing with a teen-ager.

Teen-agers just naturally think parents have no idea what is going on in the world—or out of it. At least, they give the impression of thinking this. Recognizing that this is true, that teen-agers feel this way, is a step in the right direction for a parent toward keeping communication. Refraining from fighting this attitude is perhaps the most advantageous boon to parental mental health available today. It beats Equanil and Valium by a country mile. However, having the dentist build up your teeth where you have gritted them down during the years such restraining is necessary may require a new mortgage.

Both parents and teen-agers must distinguish between communication and communion. It is possible to have communication without having communion. Communion means to share mutual ideas. Communication is the simple transmission of a message. Too often we want to make communication carry the implication of communing or agreeing. This is scarcely true. It's letting someone know how *you* feel about something. Response to messages are not always positive. Some are negative, but communication was there.

I don't know what ticky-issues parents and children will be trying to communicate about by the time this reaches its readers. But at the time I am writing this one major ticky-issue is hair, its length in particular.

To me, long stringy hair on most girls is very unbecoming. To me, extremely long hair on males is, generally speaking, tacky. But this is not enough reason for me to say to our boys that they cannot lengthen their hair a bit.

So far as I'm concerned hair is not necessarily symptomatic, so I do not feel it should be used for diagnostic purposes. I am in the minority, that's for sure.

While my personal opinion allows fine boys to have long hair, many opinions do not. Many people immediately think, hippie, drugs, laziness, rebellion, etc., when a long-haired male appears. I do not feel this way because I do not feel that short hair is indicative of good characteristics. The reason? It has been proven, in events which I *know* have happened, that some of the meanest, most destructive, most egotistical, and least tolerant-of-the-rights-of-others teen-agers around have short hair. I would not have given our boys my approval, much less my permission, to ride around the block with them. You just can't tell by the length of a fellow's hair what kind of mind and heart and behavior he has.

But, back to my point, that many things get messages across. Because we do not wish our boys to be criticized too harshly by those who prejudge long-haired youth, we do finally insist on a trip to the barbershop for a haircut. I really should say a *token* haircut, that's what it usually amounts to.

Along about the time everybody in the family knows it's getting to be that time, all we have to do is mention their barber's name or hair. In less than fifteen seconds flat James and I find ourselves in a room totally empty of boys.

That's communication.

The message they get is that part of their responsibility when we agreed to the longer hair bit was that they would keep it neat; consequently, hair is kept neater immediately following such communication. One boy said only this week, after they all finished supper surprisingly early when "barbershop" inadvertently cropped up in the conversation, "I decided I'd better start keeping my hair neater before Dad gets bothered and tells me I have to get it all cut off."

That's communication.

But it is not communion. We disagree on hair length. James and I would like the old-timey kind of haircuts; the boys like longer hair. One of them said he thinks ears are ugly and if hair can cover up ears, it should. That's not stupid just because a teen-ager said it. I took a good long look at ears from my vantage point in the choir the other Sunday, and I'm inclined to agree. Ear lobes really aren't very pretty. I expect if they were not necessary to our hearing, many of us would have them lifted (removed, you know, like a thief does to money and jewels).

Folks are constantly communicating. Each member of every family has signals by which we may get a message from him. Start watching, and even make a list, of the various ways you can interpret the moods of your mate or child, the good ones as well as the bad ones. It's amazing how well you can know your family members if you really give it a try. Study them quietly for a couple of weeks and see.

Words are sometimes the poorest ways of getting a message through. Talk is necessary, vital even. But human beings sometimes cover up their real feelings by saying what they feel the other person wants them to say.

This is a kind of dishonesty, really. While it is true that the truth does not always have to be told, it is also true that solving problems by verbal communication requires truthful verbal communication.

If a wife blows the golf plans of a husband's Saturday morning by telling the children they'll have a trip to the zoo, the husband does not really feel it is all right, so he shouldn't docilely say, "That's all right." He should express himself in a decent, adult, honest opinion and suggest they find a way to makc their plans with each other's knowledge and approval so that conflicts won't happen.

How to resolve the immediate conflict? Seems to me a Christian daddy would value his child's respect and opinion more than that of his golf buddies, who are, after all, grown up and can play golf by themselves, while nobody can take kids to the zoo like Mommy *and* Daddy.

I know that's true. When our boys were small we lived close enough to a good zoo to find it necessary to carry the boys on an expedition or two each year. James and I always took them together and made a family event out of it.

During the childhood years it seemed that the boys sort of took the zoo trips for granted. At the same time, they couldn't wait to go the first time each year, so we doggedly took them every year.

Now we are glad that we did. One of them who went on a teen-agers picnic to the zoo in that city recently came home and told us he really enjoyed the picnic. One of the reasons, he said, was that it reminded him of the trips we made to take them to the zoo when they were small.

James and I remember those trips as hot, the zoo as stinky, the cotton candy as sticky, the animals as sort of inferior, and the boys as getting tired and fussy before the day was over.

That is not the way it is stored up in the three memories for which the trips were made. You never know what things hang in a child's mind as worthy of remembrance. You never know when a child is going to need to reach into the backside of his mind and find a memory to warm him up and keep him going. It is the parents' job to be sure that memories are there and that their quality is good.

Back to communication, be sure you use the words you use in communication with youth in the light of youth's interpretation. "He scratched off" definitely does not mean "He removed it with his fingernails."

Besides knowing the current definitions of words, you have to watch semantics. A trip to the nearest dictionary, sometimes stealthily, sometimes militantly, may be necessary to assure your child (and yourself) that you know what you are talking about.

Because most of us are sort of holed up in ourselves, we find it a bit hard to really listen to others. Understanding the older generation is harder for the younger generation than understanding the younger generation is for the older one. It is the younger one's first time around. We older ones have already been there—we had silly lingo, music different from the bunch before us and after us, utterly hilarious fashion fads and unbelievable hair styles. We've already argued with our parents about injustice, politics, war, music, dating, hair, curfew, freedom. We've been through the whole bit.

Some of us refuse to remember. It's easier to shake our heads in a disgruntled wondering why kids can't behave the way they used to. That's about what they are doing. We hated and loved, blamed and defended, doubted and believed, cried and laughed. That's the way kids are doing today, the average, typical ones, I mean. All of us realize a segment of youth has itself out on a limb it doesn't know how to return from.

The things which appeal to or bother teen-agers have little interest to adults, but our interest in the teen-agers should make us take the time to listen, sympathize, encourage, whatever the youth has need of. As much as youth looks forward to the future, the present is what he really understands. It is very difficult for a young person to evaluate his behavior today in the light of what he wants to be ten years from now.

Talk with young folks about things that do not require agreement or disagreement. Every conversation you have should not involve someone's having to be persuaded about some issue. That sets the atmosphere before you get started if persuasive conversation is the only kind you ever have.

And, remember, nothing beats good listening.

Parents have moods. So do teen-agers. Don't be intimidated by their moods. They probably have little to do with us—except that we are their dumb parents. The moods have to do with them, not us. We must not allow ourselves to be hurt or to feel responsible for their moods.

It is important that parents know what and how their children are thinking—not that we'll understand *why* they are thinking that way. Sometimes quiet talks will let me know, but, if I can't find out what ours are thinking any other way, I pick an argument with them.

In an argument I can get my opinions in, too. They expect me to refute whatever of their ideas I feel disagreement with. Then they must think through my opinions in the light of theirs. This works the other way once in a while, too, I'll have to admit. I have to think through their opinions in the light of mine.

They never say at the end of an argument, "OK. You win. You've persuaded me to your opinion." I'd lose consciousness if one did.

But there is tomorrow, and there is next year.

And today's arguments may be won one of those times or somewhere between or beyond them.

We have a good friend who enjoys asking young folks, "What are you going to be if you grow up?" This query is good for a smile or two every time.

After I got past the chuckle in it, the question grabbed me where it hurts. From the time our children get here we are constantly protecting them. I have to be honest to say I have overprotected mine on occasions.

You won't believe this. One night I was leaning over the bathtub checking the warmth of the bath water I was running. This water was not for me, mind you, but for our firstborn who was then seven years old. For seven years I had been running his bath water, and for five years and three months I had been running the second-born's. That night I stood up, brushed my hair back with the back of my wrist and said to myself: This is absurd. These kids have sense enough to know when the water is too hot.

I called them in and conducted a class on how to run bath water. How can a fellow grow up when his mother won't even let him exercise his sense of touch, much less his reasoning abilities about how much hot water to use?

There's more to this incident than meets the eye. You see, for years I was an everything-in-its-place and everything-at-its-time mother—the boys never had to look for anything or wonder what to do next. Good ole Mommy was organized to the hilt and functioned accordingly, brandishing an invisible whip made of the golden thread of what I called love. What the threads really were was foolishness—I was spoiling the boys and placing them in a precarious position of having their working and thinking laid out for them. It isn't good to let someone do all your thinking for you, whether you're parent or child.

Our two oldest are twenty-one months apart. When they were tiny, they played together real well and had a good friendship going. At night they would lie in their beds and talk and talk and talk. It seemed to me that they should run out of conversation material long before they did, so I decided to listen one night to see what they were talking about. That particular night Bobby was explaining the virtues of deep-sea fishing over pool-bank fishing. Where he got his dubious information I did not ask. I stole quietly away and let them talk.

When Bobby started to school Frank became a problem during school hours. In the afternoons and on weekends he was his usual, happy, occasionally ornery, cheerful self. It took me a few weeks to realize that Frank was so accustomed to having Bobby make their plans for playing (with the aforementioned help from me) that he had no idea what to do with himself without Bobby to think and plan for them both. It took only a short time to help him learn to plan his day all for himself.

Frank's learning to think for himself brought on a few disagreements with Bobby about afternoon and weekend plans, but it was necessary for Frank's well-being that he be able to exercise his mind and will.

If a child is to grow up, he must be allowed to. The woman's dilemma comes in deciding what to allow the child to decide. Decisions seem to fall into roughly three categories: those which affect physical safety, those which affect moral safety, and those which concern life's little mundane matters.

In all these categories children and teen-agers are defenseless against grown-ups who insist on invading their realm and making all the decisions and then insisting that their own decisions be accepted.

It isn't easy for a mamma to keep herself in her place. Sometimes I have to say: "Get back in the bleachers, Mamma. You're not up to bat."

Then when I climb back into the bleachers I have to say to myself, "Quit yelling, 'Throw it to third!' You're not playing center field."

Oh, it is hard to face them—those times when you have no choice but to back off and watch your child to see if he has accepted as his the opinion or idea or conviction that you have been trying to pound into his mind and heart ever since he came to live at your house.

I often have the same sort of feeling today that I had before recitals when I was a girl. I reached such a state of nerves that if I ate food the day of a recital, I was likely to lose it. Today, with three sons in residence and bursting with life, it seems that I face a steady wave of "recitals."

I used to ask why we had to have recitals, anyway, and what recitals were for. I thought they were dumb show-off times. Now I know that they were the times when the fruition of all those hours of practice required by a teacher and a mother, sometimes almost at paddle-point, was plucked for enjoyment; but most of all, recitals were for a sense of achievement and growth.

Just so, now, these times when I stand back, nervous and anxious about the performance of our children in living—as I see each try his wings, flapping them sometimes falteringly but, more often, steadily.

All the time we are holding our children to us we must be pushing them away. This is love. Sometimes it makes us feel two-headed or schizophrenic.

There are a couple of basic things parents and children need to decide about and agree upon at the outset. The first is what parents are and the second is what children are. These may have to be adjusted as time goes along. I have concluded that our children want us to know what is going on and want us to be up-to-date and to enjoy living completely, but they do not want us to act like kids about it.

You know, when we were first exposed to teen-age music of present-day vintage, we thought we would never get accustomed to its loudness, beat, etc. But first thing we know, we will be snapping our fingers or tapping our feet or skipping a step or two with the music. Every time this happens in the presence of our boys, they act as if we just suggested they be cremated alive—they are horrified at our display of a little rhythm. They want us to act the way they think adults should act, and they'll act their age. Most children like grown-ups. I remember when I visited aunts and uncles who treated me like adults should treat a child, considering me an alert, intelligent being, feeding my sense of humor and helping me to enjoy adult company. They made no effort to act childish and made no effect to elevate me to adulthood. We just sort of met each other where each of us was and had a good time without straining.

Teen-agers really don't think they know everything—they wish they did. They are always asking us adults something if we will just listen. All they want is an intelligent answer to their question, not a case history, not a researched and documented oration, not verbosity or windiness—sometimes they don't even want a word.

They ask us by watching us. They hear us by seeing us. They want to know what we think, how we feel about anything and everything under the sun, even if they don't ask us orally.

This is not to say that they will believe immediately the same way we feel, or that they ever will. But the way we feel gives them a place to start. They must deal with what we believe. Either by disproving it or accepting it as valid.

Hopefully, our beliefs will be valid enough for acceptance as truth. More hopefully, our opinions will be worthy of acceptance as a part of the store of their maturing minds.

Children in a family probably worry about a lot of things they would not have to worry about if parents would take the time and expend the energy to explain.

Even if there is something a child should worry about, it might, in many cases, be within the ability of the child to understand what the source of worry is. The perception of small children—teen-agers, too, for that matter—is much keener than we give them credit for.

I cannot remember a time since the boys at our house began to communicate with us—and that's right after they're born—when they have not wanted to know, "What's wrong?"

Before they could speak the words, they could ask by a puzzled expression, a bid for attention, a whimper of uneasiness, all kinds of indications that everything was not just right and they knew it.

Every worry and fear should be dealt with so a child knows what is going on. This gives him a basis on which to build faith and trust.

Probably the greatest need a child has is to be wanted. Almost any difficulty is endurable if a person doesn't feel in the way.

Probably no feeling in the world is as desolate as feeling unwanted.

Maybe the next greatest need a child has is to know himself for what he really is and then to know he is accepted for himself, respected. How do you respect a child? Receive him, do not reject him. Try to like him, too. Let him have privacy. Let him think out loud without fear of being laughed at. Ask his opinion, desires, even advice. Don't allow shadows of brothers and sisters to haunt him. Compliment him on his progress. Allow him to accept whatever responsibility he wishes to try. Give him some money and time all his own.

Another great need of a child is that he learn to feel joy and hope when he thinks about the future. He needs a faith of his own. This includes a concept of God as complete as his age and ability allow him to have. You're just the one to help him here.

What makes it possible for you to teach your child about God? First, a clear concept of your own about God. Second, finding the time. Third, feeling enough at home with God to talk about him. Fourth, at least a basic knowledge of the Bible. Fifth, keeping life's values in proper perspective. Sixth, correct reaction to all the balls and strikes life throws to you.

Teach your child that God has first claim on his life, that God's plan includes more than income, comfort, ease, and the like.

When a young person is making a decision about his vocation, make it possible for him to accept the fact that he may change his mind several times before God's will is finally known. Such remarks as, "Oh, last week you were going to teach. Now, this week you're going to be an accountant. Wonder what you'll decide next week" do not help the already unsure, undecided young man.

On the other hand, if he does settle on some vocation for several months, don't make such an issue of it that he'll be embarrassed to say he's changed his mind. Of course, long about the end of the sophomore year or beginning of the junior year of college a fellow needs to show signs of a firm decision, but in high school and early college frequent changes are fairly normal.

Maybe if we did not rush our young folks so about this matter there would be more people happy with what they are doing. Too, maybe there would not be so many families facing crises of conflict and unhappiness as the adults in the family move from one kind of job to another.

Part of the difficulty in being an adolescent is in feeling inadequate. What kind of failures does a teen-ager have? Maybe a better qualification would be in order. Many things we call failures really should be called disappointments, not failures. Expecting from a teen-ager something he cannot give does not make him a failure when he cannot give it. You have a disappointment, but he doesn't have a failure.

Some areas of failure or disappointment are inability to make or keep friends, lack of achievement in school work, loss of sweetheart; more serious ones are drug or alcohol troubles, venereal disease, pregnancy, inability to handle finances wisely. You could name others because youngsters you know have had them. Our concern here, though, is not to list all of the things that can happen to a youngster for a parent to be haunted by.

But we are concerned with what a parent is supposed to do when his child makes one of the bold, glaring mistakes the parent thought his child had sense enough not to make. I guess all of us start out feeling adolescence will not happen to our children. Then suddenly we feel a need to yell: "Help! Adolescence *has* happened to my child, in spite of all I could do."

What do our children need from us when they have goofed (or when we have goofed, possibly, by allowing them freedom they were not ready for)? Presuming that we have tried to teach them to live by Christian principles, what they need from us at a time like this is a display of those Christian principles at work.

What's the greatest Christian principle? Love. Sounds good, but how do you show love to a kid you're struggling to keep from knocking upside the head? What is so wrong with saying (even if it is through gritting teeth) to your child: "I love you, boy, but I'm too furious to deal with this properly right now. We'll get together in just a little while."

Best not deal with the problem until the impulse to brow-beat has passed.

It may be that several hours cooling off before getting to the nitty-gritty will make the whole thing more approachable. Getting the facts may take this long, and facts are necessary.

I remember one day when one of our boys was whipping our family dog in what I thought was an unmerciful way for no good reason. I called him in and punished him without listening to his explanation. Embarrassment colored me red later when he showed me his All-Star baseball cap which the puppy had chewed nearly to shreds.

Nothing quite takes the place of understanding a situation.

After love, after understanding, what then?

If there is a monumental problem created by the disappointment or failure, the next thing is help to work it out as best it can be worked out.

Facing reality is absolutely necessary. You don't have to announce to the world the reality of what has happened, but everyone involved should face reality and deal squarely with it.

We could talk about hypothetical cases here or I could get permission to change names and talk about actual cases, but I see no need to. Whatever trouble happens to your child is unique and must be dealt with uniquely and by people who know how to help if it is beyond parental ability. A lot of things are. Failure to get proper help early enough usually compounds the problem.

Somewhere in all this should be forgiveness, if it is necessary. If your forgiveness is not necessary, God's is. You must show your child what to do with his problem: take it to God, ask his forgiveness, his peace, and his direction in the solving of it, his strength for future temptations. A child must learn that one bad mistake does not ruin his life, nor yours. He must know that he isn't perfect, but he must keep trying.

How about successes and accomplishments of your children? Help them enjoy them, but keep them in proper place. He is to be a good steward of his abilities and use them for the honor of the Lord. As you teach him how to do this, you will be teaching him how to have a happy life.

I am a firm believer that many teen-agers have problems, failures, and are disappointments because they are not given enough adult help to get ready for life. They beg for privileges they are not ready to handle, are allowed them, and foul up gloriously many times.

How does a family find a happy balance between freedom for and control over the young people in the home? Discussion and talking about it helps a lot. Children need to accept the truth that fear is a factor here, more than a failure to trust. There are some freedoms a fifteen-year-old feels old enough for and demands to have. The parent remembers being fifteen. He also thinks about things that have been happening to and by fifteen-year-olds in the community. The parent wonders if a fifteen-year-old needs enough freedom to put himself in a position he may not yet be ready to handle.

It may take on proportions of a major battle, this demand for freedom by the child and the exercise of control by the parents.

At the outset parents ought to agree on ground rules. If a child senses disagreement between parents on an issue, he'll play it for all it's worth.

Ground rules mustn't be the kind that break, but the kind that bend. We do not allow children to wait until they are old enough to know that going to the dentist is a wise, healthful thing to do to let them decide to go. Nor do we allow a five-year-old the privilege of playing with the car. Children do not need to be allowed to make decisions they are not yet ready to make. Some decisions must be made for them. That is the reason for house rules, or ground rules, whatever you wish to call them.

Teen-agers want some guidelines. These seem reasonable for a home with teen-agers.

1. Clear plans with parents before finalizing them.
2. Let parents know where you are and with whom.
3. Get in on the time agreed on according to situation.
4. No borrowing without permission of owner.
5. Respect privacy of a closed door, even the little guy's.
6. Keep room reasonably neat according to family policy.
7. Enter into financial deals only after consultation with Dad.

These rules are rather general, but almost any situation that could come up is included somewhere. Parents are footing for a teen-ager—footing to stand on, footing to reach from, footing to push against, footing to rest on. ("My parents won't let me," he belligerently tells his friends, and "Am I glad!" he secretly tells himself.)

There is more to life than high school. A parent needs to help a child get through adolescence with as few scars as possible. Many adolescents cannot recognize pending disaster. Sheltering is too much guidance. Protecting is what we're aiming at. A child should not be sheltered from dishonesty—he needs to know it exists, but by helping him learn how to deal with it, we help him to be protected from it.

A woman must try to help her family remove itself from as much pressure as possible. Most of us dedicated Christians have an exalted opinion of our strength and position. We are tempted to feel that because we are Christians we, nor our children who are Christians, will never bend to pressure. This is not true. There are circumstances we should not let ourselves get into.

It helps to know that teen-agers feel deeply about things: the mess the world is in—poverty, war, the draft, racial disturbances, injustice, dishonesty; the seeming irrelevance of school; suspicion of and rebellion against that nebulous entity called "the establishment"; their health; their sexuality. Their feelings are not casual. They are intense and demanding.

It also helps to know something about how teen-agers are. They are daydreamers. Sometimes they are hesitant, sometimes impulsive. They are often cynical about people and their motives. They are moody, sometimes depressed, fearful. Often they startle themselves with their efforts toward independence.

A fellow (or a girl) has one big job facing him when he is a teen-ager. He hears all kinds of things from every side. In the midst of all the voices, which often disagree about the things that bother youth most, the young person must make some very tough decisions which carry some very heavy responsibility.

Suddenly he must look at himself as a real person, after all. He is at the place where his own identity keeps trying to forge itself. He has to help decide who he is. All his life he has been pretty well doing what adults said was the thing to do. Now he begins to wonder if what he has been told and the guidance he has been given are trustworthy.

He looks around and sees others who have been told something else and have received other guidance. Who gets along better with his advice and guidance, your boy or his acquaintances? That's what he wonders, too.

It may take your adolescent a while to decide. Brace yourself. Everything you've heard about this "Who am I?" period in a young person's life is true. It is rough for parents, but it is rougher for the young person. Can't you remember it from your own teen-ager years?

Youth is not the carefree time we adults like to say it is. It just isn't. There is really not a group of more vicious people in the world than teen-agers. Watching your own being either the victim or part of those doing the victimizing is not a happy experience.

While he is sorting himself out and separating himself from us parents, he needs at least a hundred bushels of sympathetic love every day. He doesn't want it shown, but he wants to know it is there.

When you feel like throwing up your hands and walking away from your adolescent, don't. He probably wants to walk away from himself. So you need to stay around and be whatever help he needs you to be to help him be able to live with himself. He finds himself difficult to live with, just as we find him difficult to live with.

The age of parenthood is a difficult age. Parents go through stages, too. Parents may be as taxing on the nerves of their children as children are on the nerves of parents.

Think of all the things that you worried about last week. How did they turn out? Did you need to have worried?

Considering the percentages of last week, what percentage of this week's worrying could you get along without?

Your adolescent says, "There's a whole new world out there. I'm gonna' find it!"

Help him find the good in the world out there, and you'll all be glad you did!

Her Crises

When you think of all the things that make up the complex unit we call the family, it is no wonder that crisis situations present themselves almost constantly.

A crisis time for a family means a time when something is wrong and must be worked out. Stress is present. It follows that weathering the crisis involves doing whatever will best reduce, or relieve completely, the stress.

Every crisis is not precipitated by something bad. The promotion Dad has worked for comes through. The family is elated, but crisis joins the party because the promotion means a move to another city and to a higher social level.

There really haven't been a great many new problems uncovered for families lately. However, new implications for and possible complications from problems uncover themselves all along. For instance, it is easier for the problem of sex to blossom into adultery because of travel, etc. It is easier now for the problem of tension to lead to alcoholism and drug addiction because of laxity of laws and deadening of consciences of those who deal in such traffic. Discontent can lead to disastrous over-spending, what with such ridiculously easy credit. In other words, it is much easier to suffer worse consequences from almost every problem than it was even twenty-five years ago.

I read somewhere sometime that the Chinese word for crisis comes from two words, one meaning danger and one meaning opportunity. This seems a likely coupling of root words, for each crisis really does involve danger and opportunity. Crisis properly handled is usually a strengthening force. Poorly handled, crisis weakens.

Let's mention some of the crises that come along these days.

Illness is a practically ever-present crisis. This illness may be insignificant and pesky or it may be serious. The serious illnesses come in roughly two kinds: the ones you can recover from or can control and the ones you die from.

In case of the former, the way a Christian woman faces the crisis of illness is to see that whoever is sick gets the proper medical attention and proper conditions for complete recovery or whatever convalescence is possible. It sounds simple, but it can turn a household four ways at once unless everyone involved understands that recovery from illness is the responsibility of everyone in the family.

The illnesses you die from require you to figure out how you feel about death and how you can live in a crisis situation for whatever length of time is required. It would be good if Christians could look at death easier and trust God to see that it doesn't hurt too much. The dismal cloak we have wrapped around death doesn't do too much for our Christian testimony of hope.

I would be the last to raise my hand in answer to the question, "Wouldn't you like to go on to heaven now?" But I think I could get my hand up reasonably fast to answer, "No" to "Does the thought of dying scare the daylights out of you?" A healthy attitude toward death should be part of a Christian woman's concept of God, as we have already mentioned, and she should help her family on this.

Other frequent crises have their roots in occupational situations, like unemployment, failure to get a promotion or raise, personality clashes on the job.

Then there are marital crises such as unfaithfulness, differences concerning family goals, difficulties involving children, tensions with in-laws.

Other kinds of crises include financial ones which may be temporary and easily adjusted or they may be drastic.

Social crises involving friendships, social issues, moral issues, politics all find their way to our houses.

Religious or spiritual crises often come when families fail to relate properly to God.

How should a Christian family feel about crisis? Well, you don't wait until crisis appears to get ready for it. The family member who smiles insipidly and thinks crisis happens to neighbors and foreigners is not prepared to do what must be done in crisis times.

First, you do all you can to avoid and avert crisis. Wise spending seldom results in financial crisis. Faithfulness in marriage seldom begets marital crisis. All the *right* things you do help to head-off such specialized kinds of crises.

Second, you build your faith in God by coming to see him as your power and strength in reserve. You remember, he has faced crisis, too. Look what happened to his first people. Look how ornery his chosen people act. And what crisis is greater than a Son's death?

Third, you thank God for all the lovely things of your life every day. This keeps things in perspective. If you're accustomed to looking for pretties and saying, "Thank you," to God for them, you'll be able to have something on your mind besides whatever crisis is on it.

Fourth, you remember that a crisis is not the end of the world. It may seem to be, but it really isn't. Embarrassing, heart-breaking, maddening, yes. But world-ending? No. Not even your world.

Fifth, you recognize that crisis is a fact of life—your life. When it comes, the family should face it together, as many of the family as are mature enough to do so. If any member of the family needs help no other family member can give, seek that help immediately.

Crisis will come, and crisis will go. But, you, a Christian woman, and your Christian home, will abide through it because you abide in God the Father.

Ending

Being a Christian woman in a Christian home is like icing on a cake.

Icing on a cake means many things to many people. It took me the better part of two years to triumph in making chocolate icing. One day James gravely endangered his shiny, bald head by bluntly suggesting that I quit trying. We had eaten icing with a spoon or chiseled it with a butcher knife so often he figured the case was hopeless.

But my third-grade teacher, perturbed by my giving up so easily, had made me write one hundred times, "If at first you don't succeed, try, try again." So I tried and tried again. And succeeded.

As long as we had only two boys big enough to want to scrape the boiler, the problem was easily solved—just leave a thickly-coated, half-full spoon for one and hand the boiler to the other. When the third set of hands and eyes began reaching for a spoon or boiler I had to find some excuse for ending up with two spoons in the boiler. It's been worth all the effort it took me to learn to make icing.

But the icing on the cake icing came one day when I had about decided that some icing I made might have to be eaten with spoons. However, sometime later one of the boys said, "Mamma, the icing is going to hard up."

I happened to be looking at the youngest, James Neil, when Bobby said that. He and Frank were sitting at the table awaiting the outcome of the icing in question. The most delighted expression spread over James Neil's face. His nose crinkled and his eyes sparkled. He sort of learned back and easing his breath out slowly, explained, "Ooh, that's when icing is good. When it is thick and hard and you can peel it off and lay it over at the side and eat it all by itself when you've finished the cake. Man, it's good."

I remembered how many times I had done that very thing when I was a little girl. And a delighted feeling spread over my heart.

Then it came to me that heaven will be the icing on the cake. All the time I'm eating the cake here, blessing after blessing, the hunks of icing are laid aside, waiting for me when I have finished eating the cake.

Wish I could find the fellow who said you can't have your cake and eat it, too. So I could show him that you can.

Why strive for perfection? We said that we strive because it is in the striving that we aim high and find that we need the strength and power of our Father. We strive because he instructed us to strive to be perfect as he is perfect. We strive because the more we attempt the more we accomplish. We strive because we believe in the promises of God when he promised us the righteousness of Jesus Christ and the reality of his presence for all eternity.

IT'S GONNA' BE GREAT

I'm gonna' really
>be something
>>when I get to heaven.

>Gonna' sing like Kate Smith
>>play the piano like Van Cliburn
>>cook like Betty Crocker
>>paint like Van Gogh
>>look like Miss America.

But,
>best of all,
>>I'm gonna' be like Christ.

And that, finally, will be the perfection I've been looking for all these years.